"Every believer wants to know how to fully connect with Jesus. In *Synced*, Jennifer demonstrates how the power of the Holy Spirit is accessed through a praying life and radical obedience is the result of a life in sync to the purposes and cause of Christ. If you want to know how to deepen your walk with Jesus, this book will be sure to take you there. I highly recommend it."

—NANCY McGUIRK, author of *To Live Is Christ*

"In *Synced*, Jennifer skillfully explains the desire, the determination, and the discipline we need to live in alignment with our God-given purpose. The message is profound yet practical."

—DEBORAH SMITH PEGUES, best-selling author of *30 Days to Taming Your Tongue*

"As I read Jennifer Kennedy Dean's new book, *Synced*, I thought, *Oh, that we could live in the harmony and communion with the Lord that she describes so skillfully.* And what amazing things God can do through us, His beloved children, as we are 'synced' to Jesus. Life would never be the same. Inspiring, clear, and compelling, Jennifer's book is a must read for those who want to grow in grace and prayer."

—CHERI FULLER, speaker and author of *Dangerous Prayer*, *The One Year Praying the Promises of God*, and *What A Girl Needs From Her Mom*

"Jennifer Kennedy Dean has crafted a much-needed book about a vital topic: what it means to live heart-to-heart with God through prayer. Jennifer has a gift for helping readers draw closer to Jesus, and nothing could matter more. This book can change your life! When we learn to live with God in the moment, He welcomes us into fresh discoveries of His presence, power, and love. The adventure awaits! You won't want to miss the mercies that only happen when we pray."

—DR. JAMES BANKS, author of *Prayers for Prodigals*

SYNCED

Living Connected to the Heart of Jesus

Other New Hope books by
JENNIFER KENNEDY DEAN

Set Apart

Prayer Fatigue

Conversations with the Most High

Live a Praying Life®

Live a Praying Life® *in Adversity*

Heart's Cry

Clothed with Power

Clothed with Power DVD

Power in the Blood of Christ

Power in the Name of Jesus

Altar'd

Pursuing the Christ

The Power of Small

Live a Praying Life® Bible Study—Tenth Anniversary Edition

Live a Praying Life® DVD Leader Kit—Tenth Anniversary Edition

Live a Praying Life® Journal

Life Unhindered!

Set Apart DVD Leader Kit

Secrets Jesus Shared

Secrets Jesus Shared DVD Leader Kit

JENNIFER **KENNEDY** DEAN

SYNCED

Living Connected to the Heart of Jesus

NEW HOPE®
PUBLISHERS
Gospel-Centered. Missions-Driven.

BIRMINGHAM, ALABAMA

New Hope® Publishers
PO Box 12065
Birmingham, AL 35202-2065
NewHopePublishers.com
New Hope Publishers is a division of WMU®.

New Hope Publishers serves its authors as they express their views, which may not express the views of the publisher.

Library of Congress Cataloging-in-Publication Data
Dean, Jennifer Kennedy.
  Synced : living connected to the heart of Jesus / Jennifer Kennedy Dean.
    pages cm
  ISBN 978-1-59669-466-8 (sc)
  1. Lord's prayer--Criticism, interpretation, etc. 2. Spiritual life--Christianity. I. Title.
  BV230.D355 2016
  226.9'606--dc23
                          2015034199

ISBN-10: 1-59669-466-1
ISBN-13: 978-1-59669-466-8

N164106 • 0316 • 3M1

DEDICATION

As always, to my sons and daughters-in-law:

Brantley and Caroline

Kennedy and Sara

Stinson and Stephanie

PHILIPPIANS 1:9–11

CONTENTS

Our Father in heaven,

hallowed be your name,

your kingdom come,

your will be done,

on earth as it is in heaven.

Give us today our daily bread.

And forgive us our debts,

as we also have forgiven our debtors.

And lead us not into temptation,

but deliver us from the evil one.

—MATTHEW 6:9–13

CHAPTER 1

LIVING SYNCED

The Son can do nothing by himself; he can do only what he sees his Father doing, because whatever the Father does the Son also does. For the Father loves the Son and shows him all he does.

—JOHN 5:19–20

The secret to Jesus' life of power lies in this: His heart was perfectly synced to the Father's. He had neither action nor interest that was separate from the Father's. The heart of the Son beat in unison with the heart of the Father. Though they were one in nature, this unity of interest was born of a conscious willingness on Jesus' part to live fully yielded and in unbroken obedience. Jesus *decided* to submit to the Father's will. He made a *choice* to surrender. "Not my will, but yours be done" (Luke 22:42). "For I have come down from heaven not to do my will but to do the will of him who sent me" (John 6:38).

Though Jesus had His own desires arising from His humanity, when those desires conflicted with the Father's, He always chose the Father's will. Jesus had no sinful desires because sin never had a place in His heart, but He had natural desires. In His manhood, He desired, for example, not to go to the Cross. Along the way, He had natural desires that were not sinful but at times had to be subjugated to the Father's will. On purpose and with resolve. When His natural desires conflicted with the Father's will, He had to *choose* the Father's will.

Every time He encountered a situation in which His human will and the Father's divine will differed, He bowed to the Father's desires. In Philippians 2:8, Paul writes that Jesus "humbled himself by becoming obedient to death—even death on a cross!" He went from being equal with the Father to being humbly obedient to the Father. He was obedient in everything, even to the point of dying on the Cross. The Book of Hebrews further says that He "learned obedience" (Hebrews 5:8). I addressed this in depth in *Power in the Blood of Christ*. Here is a synopsis.

> He was never disobedient, but He continually progressed to deeper levels of obedience as deeper levels were required. He progressed to the point where He could be "obedient to death—even death on a cross" (Philippians 2:8). The Father did not require the same level of obedience from 12-year-old Jesus as He did from 20-year-old Jesus. Nor did He require the same level of obedience from 20-year-old Jesus as He did from 33-year-old Jesus. God trained His Son step-by-step. He trained Him in deeper levels of obedience.

In living synced to the Father's heart, Jesus chose the Father's will over and over. Andrew Murray, in *Holiest of All*, explains this:

As the Son of God, come from heaven, one would say that there could be no thought of His learning obedience. But so real was His emptying Himself of His life in glory, and so complete was His entrance into all the conditions and likeness of our nature, that He did indeed need to learn obedience. This is of the very essence of the life of a reasonable creature, of man—that the life and the will he has received from God cannot be developed without the exercise of a self-determining power and without the voluntary giving up to God in all that He asks, even where it appears to be a sacrifice. The creature can only attain his perfection under a law of growth, of trial, and of development, in the overcoming of what is contrary to God's will and the assimilating of what that will reveals.

Living synced, then, starts with an unreserved commitment to full and undiluted obedience.

LIVING IN THE FLOW

We see the aspect of obedience that entails a deliberate choice of God's will over Jesus' human will when the two differed. But there is another aspect to obedience: the deliberate doing of the Father's desires. Accomplishing the Father's goals. Aligning with the Father's purposes. Also in Hebrews we read a quotation from the Psalms attributed to the Messiah: "Then I said, 'Here I am—it is written about me in the scroll—I have come to do your will, my God'" (Hebrews 10:7). He did what the Father showed Him to do. So, a combination of relinquishing desires when necessary, and embracing the aspirations of the Father to carry out His agenda, defined Jesus' complete obedience. His adherence to the Father's will and full surrender to His desires enabled Jesus to live synced with the Father's heart.

To live synced, Jesus had to have an intuition—an immediate knowing—of what the Father was doing. He didn't have to stop every so often to bow His head and close His eyes and ask the Father. He just walked perpetually in the power and provision of God. "For the Father loves the Son and shows him all he does" (John 5:20). Throughout this book, we will see what that looks like—this living in the flow.

The picture His intuitive and persistent obedience paints is of two so perfectly synchronized that they are one. Their movements correlate precisely. Their thoughts are integrated so that they are in tandem. Their hearts beat simultaneously.

Think synchronized swimmers. Graceful, original movements. Incredibly difficult complex choreography. Every move executed so that the myriad team members seem to be one. Almost mirror images. The beauty of the performance is in the flawless synchronization. Their seamless execution looks easy and natural.

In reality, the stunning synchronization is far from natural or easy. It is unnatural. It is contrary to what comes naturally. Their beautiful synchronicity is the result of hours and hours of work and practice, overcoming the innate inclination to act independently. No room for improvisation.

The hours of training—as much as eight to ten hours a day six days a week—is not necessary for only learning the moves. That likely comes more easily. The hours are for learning to make each move in sync with someone else. This requires far more than skill or ability. It demands that a swimmer practices the moves with her eyes glued to someone else. Moves are measured and timed so that the exact same move is being performed in the exact same way at the exact same time. The most challenging training involved is the training of the mind, essentially syncing the thoughts of several individuals until the several have become as one. The training yields a performance of many swimmers so in tandem that it seems to be natural, belying the hours of deliberate concentration and training to be in sync.

LIVING SYNCED

Even for Jesus, syncing His heart to the Father's required deliberate intention and decision. Jesus was one in nature with the Father from the beginning but was a separate being. He chose submission as the very tenor of His life but chose to obey in the moment as the moment arose.

He kept His eyes glued to the Father. I'm captured by the way Jesus uses the language of seeing to indicate how He knew His Father's will. He can only do what He *sees* His Father doing, and the Father *shows* Him everything He is doing. To live synced, Jesus never let His gaze wander. He kept the eyes of His heart locked on the Father.

As He walked out His days in step with the Father, His perfectly choreographed obedience seemed to come effortlessly. He seemed to know instinctively what the Father was doing at any given juncture. Doing the Father's will appeared to be the natural cadence of His life.

Like the synchronized swimmers, what came effortlessly at the appointed time flowed from what preceded it. The hours spent syncing His heart to the Father's in prayer were the explanation for His flowing, fluent rhythms of obedience, in step with the Father.

Prayer marked Jesus' life. Long, extended times of prayer. Spontaneous eruptions of prayer. Prayer in public, and alone with His disciples. Certainly, Jesus, who only did and spoke what the Father showed Him, did not use prayer to argue, beg, or try to change God's mind. Then why did Jesus pray? Why was prayer such a hallmark of His life that His disciples asked Him to teach them to pray like He prayed? What was He doing when He rose up early to pray or spent all night in prayer?

We might get a hint from His time in Gethsemane, where some of His words are recorded, and so we get a glimpse into the tone of His interchange with the Father. We see Him synchronizing His heart with the Father's heart.

I think it works like this: I have many mobile electronic devices that I use to accomplish my daily tasks, entertain myself, or stay in touch with others. I do most of my work on my main desktop computer, but then I need to transfer the work I've done, the information I've added, or the files I've edited from my main computer to my mobile devices. How do I accomplish that? How do I get what is on the hard drive of my computer downloaded onto my mobile devices? All those new files I created, or tweaks to existing files, are stored in the cloud. When I open one of my mobile devices, a program is activated that automatically syncs all the changes, updates, and new files. What is on my computer is reproduced on my mobile device.

In His all-night prayer in Gethsemane, we see Jesus linking His heart to the Father's. Let me summarize the content of His recorded prayer in some new words. "Father, download Your will into my heart so that it overwrites any other desire. Download courageous faith that deletes fear. Synchronize My heart's desire to Yours."

What came from that heart-to-heart transaction? Observe the Jesus who emerges from His hours of agony. Observe a Jesus who is courageous, deliberate, and marching out to meet His enemy rather than waiting to be taken. Handing Himself over to the purposes of the Father without reservation. "The hour has come. Look, the Son of Man is delivered into the hands of sinners. Rise! Let us go! Here comes my betrayer!" (Mark 14:41–42).

In response to His disciples' request to teach them to pray, He taught them the topics He addressed in prayer and the heart of those topics in a typically rabbinical style prayer we call the Model Prayer. If we move on from what the words mean and look at the effect those words produced in His life and ministry, we will see what a praying life looks like. We will see what it means to live synced. We will see how the prayers He prayed became the life He lived.

PATTERNED AFTER THE PROTOTYPE

If you keep my commands, you will remain in my love, just as I have kept my Father's commands and remain in his love.

—JOHN 15:10

One of Jesus' roles was to be the prototype of a new creation—a new kind of human being. He lived out in real time what a man synced to the Father's heart looked like. He told us the secrets of the synchronized life. He promised that the same secrets that kept Him living synced with the Father would keep us living synced with Him. He invites us to follow Him—a call that requires that we keep our eyes glued to Him, a call that speaks of being on the move, a call that says that the destination is the journey. Living synced.

JESUS' RELATIONSHIP TO THE FATHER	OUR RELATIONSHIP TO JESUS
"The Son can do nothing by himself" (John 5:19).	"Apart from me you can do nothing" (John 15:5).
The Father . . . shows him all he does" (John 5:20).	"I . . . will . . . show myself to them" (John 14:21).
"I am in the Father, and . . . the Father is in me" (John 14:10).	"If you remain in me and I in you" (John 15:5).
"The Father may be glorified in the Son" (John 14:13).	"Glory has come to me through them" (John 17:10).
"Just as the Father knows me and I know the Father" (John 10:15).	"I know my sheep and my sheep know me" (John 10:14).

Embedded in the prayer outline Jesus offered His disciples is the blueprint for how Jesus kept His life synced. The key lies not so much in the words themselves but in the way His articulated prayer was fleshed out in His life and activity, in the way His prayer life became His praying life.

LIVE A PRAYING LIFE

Jesus lived a praying life. Prayer was not an activity with set boundaries and assigned wording but a way of walking in the power and provision of the Father every minute of every day.

I have been learning about, teaching about, and writing about a praying life for several decades now. It is the grid through which I have come to view life. It has been so transformative for me that I have spent all my adult life sharing the concept with others. I still remember when the phrase came to me and recalibrated everything in my understanding. Not "have a prayer life" but "live a praying life."

Jesus knows what makes prayer work, and He is perfectly willing to teach us the secret. In my own life, as I replaced the thought of saying prayers—sandwiching words between "dear God" and "amen"—with the awareness of being in the flow of His power and provision, I expanded my definition of prayer. Now it includes the continual interaction between the material and the spiritual realm—sometimes articulated, but often simply an inarticulate flow between His heart and mine.

A praying life, then, is flowing continually. Prayer is an ongoing pursuit. Rather than start, stop, pick up where you left off, it just moves from one level to another in your multitasking mind. Yet this praying life is undergirded and nourished by daily times of concentrated prayer.

> *Very early in the morning, while it was still dark, Jesus got up, left the house and went off to a solitary place, where he prayed.*
>
> —MARK 1:35

At daybreak, Jesus went out to a solitary place.

—LUKE 4:42

One day Jesus was praying in a certain place. When he finished . . .

—LUKE 11:1

One of those days Jesus went out to a mountainside to pray, and spent the night praying to God.

—LUKE 6:12

After he had dismissed them, he went up on a mountainside by himself to pray. Later that night, he was there alone.

—MATTHEW 14:23

THE PRAYER TEACHER

A praying life is a life lived on earth in the power of heaven.
The earthly life of Jesus demonstrates this paradox. The Son of Man lived every earthly moment in the power from on high. He lived a praying life. In and through Jesus, heaven invaded earth. His obedient praying life was the conduit through which heaven's power changed earth's circumstances. He lived and moved and had His being (Acts 17:28) in the atmosphere of the spiritual realm, though He walked out His life as a man tethered to earth just like we are. From the heavenly realms, He drew His energy and power, accessed wisdom and insight, secured peace and joy. He lived out of heaven's

resources for the daily demands of earth's circumstances. He lived in the flow of God's power and provision.

He alone can teach us to pray, and He alone can reproduce His praying life in us. His praying life, indwelling us and flowing through us like the vine's life flows through the branch, is the source of our praying lives.

SYNCED TO THE SPIRIT

Paul writes; "Since we live by the Spirit, let us keep in step with the Spirit" (Galatians 5:25). The phrase *keep in step* makes me think of a march or dance. Where my foot lands is determined by where another's foot has landed. Eugene Peterson interprets Galatians 5:25 like this in *The Message*:

> *Since this is the kind of life we have chosen, the life of the Spirit, let us make sure that we do not just hold it as an idea in our heads or a sentiment in our hearts, but work out its implications in every detail of our lives.*

Keep in step with the Spirit, who is the life of Jesus indwelling you in present-tense power, imparting His very energy and impulses to each step we take. Does it sound exciting? Or impossible?

God does not issue a command for which He does not supply power. If He commands us to keep in step with the Spirit, then we can read that as His promise that He will empower us to do so. He does not intend that our Christian walk should be a struggle or a burden. Instead, He offers rest for our souls. Living in step with Him means living at rest.

For years I have been describing this walk as a praying life. To me, it means a dimension of living where your daily, minute-by-minute experience is walking in the flow of God's provision. You are met at every step with the progressive unfolding of His tailor-made plan for your life (Ephesians 2:10). You cease your struggle to find the will of God because the will of God has found you.

Every moment is pregnant with purpose. Every moment is drenched in power. Prayer is no longer the means by which you attempt to get God to perform for you and becomes, instead, the means by which you connect with His heart and mind. A praying life is a life of peace and soul rest.

Here's the secret: the praying life is Jesus. He lives in you. He is longing to express His praying life through you. He is the one and only Praying Life, and He is living in you. Andrew Murray, in his book *With Christ in the School of Prayer*, explains it this way:

> We do this because we are partakers of His life—"Christ is our life"; "No longer I, but Christ liveth in me." The life in Him and in us is one and the same. His life in heaven is an *ever-praying* life. When it descends and takes possession of us . . . in us too it is the *ever-praying* life—a life that without ceasing asks and receives from God. . . . As we know that Jesus communicates His whole life in us, He also out of that prayerfulness which is His alone, breathes into us our praying.

Jesus says that when we *learn from Him*, we will find rest for our souls. He will teach us His secret for living synced, and when we learn His secret, we will find escape from our wearying anxiety, shame, worry, anger, and every other burden weighing us down.

> *Come to Me, all who are weary and heavy-laden, and I will give you rest. Take My yoke upon you and* learn from Me, *for I am gentle and humble in heart, and* YOU WILL FIND REST FOR YOUR SOULS.
>
> —MATTHEW 11:28–29 (NASB, author's emphasis)

What did those who observed Him day-by-day, minute-by-minute, recognize as the key to His joy, His confidence, and His soul rest?

"One day Jesus was praying in a certain place. When he finished, one of his disciples said to him, 'Lord, teach us to pray'" (Luke 11:1). The implied end of that request is "like you pray." His answer to how He prays is what we call the Model Prayer.

His life of power and confidence had its roots in His life of prayer. In *Synced*, we will explore the Model Prayer from this vantage point:

- First, what did each petition mean to Jesus? He claimed these to be the topics He prayed, by which He synced His heart with the Father's.

- Second, how can we see that petition working itself out in Jesus' daily life? How did God's "yes" to that particular petition take on flesh? The Gospel accounts of Jesus' earthly life show us that Jesus

found Himself in the right place at the right time without struggling and agonizing.

I will include real-life stories of people living connected to the heart
of Jesus, finding themselves in the right place at the right time.

I'm not attempting to write an exegesis of the Model Prayer but,
rather, to use the petitions of the prayer as the anchor points for the
way Jesus lived His life in step with the Father, and how we can live
our lives in step with the Spirit.

The first breakthrough understanding about prayer is that there
is no recipe to follow or "ten easy steps" to power in prayer. Power
praying does not require that you master a skill but that you pursue a
present-tense relationship with the living and indwelling Jesus.

"Lord, teach me to pray" is not a cry for better words to say or
a better order to put them in. Rather it is a heart cry to learn to
pray like He prays. To tap in to a flowing undercurrent of prayer that
puts me smack-dab in the middle of the good works God prepared
in advance for me to do (Ephesians 2:10). To align my heart with
His so fully that I instinctively act in ways that fulfill His purposes
(Philippians 2:13). I want Jesus to teach me to live synced to His
heart.

CHAPTER 2

THE ART OF PRAYER

Jesus, during His earthly ministry, was a rabbi. *Rabbi* had a specific meaning. It meant one who was trained and educated in Scripture and whose life and livelihood was the teaching of Scripture to disciples. Jesus was recognized as a rabbi among His contemporaries. No one disputed the title when He was addressed as such. He was afforded the prerogatives of a rabbi, like teaching in the synagogue, being an honored guest in homes, being invited to banquets, and amassing crowds who traveled to hear Him teach.

He was noted as an *extraordinary* rabbi. When Rabbi Jesus taught, other rabbis and scholars—men whose whole lives consisted of studying and teaching and who listened to numerous teachers year after year—were astounded at His teaching. Astounded! Left speechless. "The Jews were amazed and asked, 'How did this man get such learning without having been taught?'" (John 7:15). The leading scholars and opinion shapers were amazed. They were all the more amazed because He had such learning without having studied with a rabbi.

No controversy on this point. This man, formally credentialed or not, was a rabbi in the full sense of the word. "The people were amazed at his teaching, because he taught them as one who had authority, not as the teachers of the law" (Mark 1:22). Other experts and rabbis backed their teaching with the teaching of rabbis before them. But Rabbi Jesus, because God Himself was His rabbi, proclaimed eternal truth with power and authority. Something in His delivery, and in the very words He spoke, found a target in the hearts of His listeners and struck a chord of truth.

In an incident toward the end of Jesus' earthly life, the religious leaders sent the temple guards to arrest Him. Now, think about this. Temple guards were accustomed to taking people into custody. They had encountered people who resisted them or tried to escape them. It's what they do. But they returned without Jesus in tow. Here is the description of that moment:

> Finally the temple guards went back to the chief priests and the Pharisees, who asked them, "Why didn't you bring him in?" "No one ever spoke the way this man does," the guards replied.
>
> —JOHN 7:45–46

They didn't say that He had outrun them or outmaneuvered them. They were held back by the very power of His person and the words He spoke with such authority. They were temple guards. They had heard many spellbinding preachers, charismatic teachers, and respected rabbis. But they had never heard the very Word of God speaking the words of God. They had never heard anything like it. It stopped them in their tracks.

Without question, Jesus was a rabbi, recognized as such by His peers. Like all rabbis, He chose disciples. Each rabbi had a group of disciples who traveled with him, not only acquiring knowledge from the rabbi but also learning from his life. A rabbi might have a large group of disciples who accompanied him, but he had a hand-selected few from that group who were his elite. These were the ones who stayed with him day and night and who were the recipients of his innermost thoughts and ideas. The larger group of disciples might follow for a while and then return home. Their ranks changed from day to day. But those in the inner circle devoted their lives to this particular rabbi. The rabbi's goal was to reproduce himself in his disciples so that they thought what he thought but also thought *as he thought*. They reasoned the way he reasoned and came at a passage of Scripture as he did. By having front-row seats to a rabbi's life, the disciples began to reflect his character. They conformed their habits and speech to his. A disciple did more than simply hear his rabbi. He observed his rabbi.

TAKE MY YOKE, AND LEARN FROM ME

Come to me, all you who are weary and burdened, and I will give you rest. Take my yoke upon you and learn from me, for I am gentle and humble in heart, and you will find rest for your souls. For my yoke is easy and my burden is light.

—MATTHEW 11:28–30

In the rabbinical system, there were different schools of rabbinical thought, and these schools, or ways of approaching interpretation of the Torah, were called "yokes." To become a disciple of one rabbi or another was to take that particular rabbi's yoke "upon your neck." Rabbis debated one another, and their disciples debated the disciples of other rabbis. They wore different "yokes."

When Jesus' contemporaries heard Him invite them to take His yoke upon them, there was no confusion about what He meant. "Take my yoke upon you and learn *from* me" (v. 29, author's emphasis) He said. A disciple did not learn *about* his rabbi. He learned *from* his rabbi. A disciple was not a casual learner; rather, he was one who left everything else in order to follow his rabbi day and night.

A rabbi tried to teach his disciples everything he knew. He wanted to pour into his disciples all of his knowledge and wisdom. Jesus said to His disciples, "Everything that I learned from my Father I have made known to you" (John 15:15). Everything! Do you see the heart of a rabbi? When a disciple was fully taught, he would be like his rabbi or teacher. Jesus put it this way: "The student [disciple] is not above the teacher [Jesus would likely have used the word *rabbi* as that is His role with His disciples], but everyone who is fully trained [disciple] will be like their teacher [rabbi]" (Luke 6:40, author's words added). Again, a rabbi's intention was to teach his disciples everything he knew and reproduce himself in his disciples. Do you see it here?

> You call me "Teacher" and "Lord," and rightly so, for that is what I am. Now that I, your Lord and Teacher, have washed your feet, you also should wash one another's feet.

I have set you an example that you should do as I have done for you.

—JOHN 13:13–15

The disciple should do and become everything his rabbi taught him and modeled for him.

It was customary for a rabbi to teach his disciples to pray. It was expected. It was part of the curriculum. They had many formulaic prayers that were said in certain settings at certain times of day, but each rabbi would teach a more personal form of the standard prayers to his disciples. Notice how Jesus' disciples included in their request that He teach them to pray, "Just as John taught his disciples" (Luke 11:1). It was a rabbi's job to teach his disciples to pray like he prayed. They taught index prayers, or bullet point prayers, exactly like the form of Jesus' Model Prayer. These rabbi-taught prayers got to the heart of what the rabbi believed significant, and they encapsulated the topics he felt to be essential. How a rabbi taught his disciples to pray said much about the heart of the rabbi.

Knowing that, it catches my attention that Jesus' disciples had to ask Him to teach them to pray. Why wasn't that lesson number one? We have already looked at the central role that prayer played in Jesus' life, so why wasn't prayer the primary lesson? Why wasn't prayer the first thing He poured into them?

Could it be that He wanted them to be hungry to know how to pray? He wanted them to have seen the effect of prayer and to have observed prayer's role in His life and ministry so that when they asked Him to teach them to pray, they were not asking just for the sake of being informed or increasing their knowledge or advancing their standing as disciples. He wanted to teach them to pray when the desire to pray like their rabbi had grown in them to become a thirst that had to be quenched. He wanted them to have developed an insatiable appetite for prayer.

By being with Him long enough and through many and varied situations, they had opportunity to observe a direct correlation between prayer and power, a direct link from the time spent alone with the Father to the unflappable peace that carried Him, the nexus of prayer and the joy that was the hallmark of His life (see John 15:11).

By the time they asked Him specifically to teach them to pray, they were primed exactly as Jesus wanted them to be. They couldn't wait any longer. They couldn't be patient until their rabbi got around to teaching them to pray. It became a burning desire that could not be held in. It was more than wanting to know how to say good prayers. They wanted to know how to live with prayer as the fulcrum of their lives. It was the kind of living that flowed from praying that they longed to experience. Like their rabbi.

TEACHING PRAYER

Jesus gave His disciples instruction in praying. The essential portion of the instruction was how He lived, not what He said. But He gave them words in which to express the aspect of prayer that is articulated. These were not words that have to be repeated verbatim but, rather, a guide, model, or outline. Likely, Jesus would have expanded on each of the topics in His index prayer during other times of in-depth teaching. Rabbis taught their disciples in ways that made it easier for them to memorize because memorization is how they learned. They didn't have textbooks or writing utensils with which to take notes. They had to memorize. So, the form of index prayer was a typical way to teach the main points.

Keeping in mind that Jesus and His disciples spent 24 hours a day together, we know we don't have a record of every word Jesus said to them. You can imagine that they talked many hours about prayer and that they prayed together with Jesus and each other. We have only a few recorded prayers of Jesus. We have the two versions of His Model Prayer from two different settings. Matthew's version was in the context of Jesus' inaugural sermon that we often refer to as the Sermon on the Mount and was part of a teaching on how the kingdom of God operates. It was addressed to the crowds. Luke's version is Jesus' response to His disciples' plea to teach them to pray like He, their rabbi, prays. It is addressed to His disciples in an intimate setting. We have Jesus' prayer recorded in John 17, His prayer as He contemplated the change that was about to occur in His ministry. He was about to leave the physical presence of His beloved disciples and transition to being with them through His indwelling presence communicated by His Spirit. We also have some of His prayer in Gethsemane as He faced His execution. Other than those, we have records of short, spontaneous prayers that give great insight into the content of His prayers, as they are the overflow of His heart. Each of these recorded prayers teach us much about prayer, and we see His prayers lived out as He walked the earth and interacted with the flawed and ragged personalities of those He came to save.

The Jesus present-in-flesh-and-blood man during His days on earth is the very same Jesus present to us by His indwelling Spirit. In fact, Jesus told His disciples that He would be more present to them through His Spirit than He was in the earthly body that was His temporary habitation.

He told His disciples that it was to their advantage that He "go away," or leave their physical sight. "But very truly I tell you, it is for your good that I am going away. Unless I go away, the Advocate will not come to you; but if I go, I will send him to you" (John 16:7). He told them that by His indwelling Spirit, He would be with them in such a way that He would never leave them or forsake them (Hebrews 13:5). He wouldn't leave them for one single nanosecond. He is with them always. All the time. Everywhere. *Always* (Matthew 28:20). Not for a heartbeat would He be separate from them in this new arrangement where, by His Spirit, He made His home in them. What He explained to His disciples is the truth for all His followers forever. True for you and for me.

If Jesus was willing and eager to teach His disciples to pray like He prays while He was in His earthly ministry, then He is equally eager to teach us to pray right now. In fact, He can teach us from inside better than He could teach the disciples who could hear Him with physical ears and see Him with physical eyes. The Spirit of Truth, whose job it is to teach us all things, lives in us with direct access to our minds and hearts (John 14:26; 16:13). Jesus, through His Spirit in us, will joyfully teach us to pray.

When you want to learn something, you want to learn from the best. If you can learn from the master, the one who instigated and established the discipline you want to understand, all the better. Who knows the ins and outs of any skill better than the one who first established it? You and I have the great privilege of learning from the Master Pray-er, the One who instigated prayer from the beginning and designed it so that it works as He means for it to work. He knows the intricacies and the potential roadblocks. He established and pioneered prayer. He wants to be our Rabbi and to teach us everything He knows about prayer.

Not only does He know all about prayer, but He knows all about us. He knows every detail about each one of us. He knows how we learn and what our bent is and what it will take to teach any one of us exactly what we need to know to live the abundant life He promised. He knows what lies behind that has colored our perceptions of prayer and of Him, and He knows what lies ahead that will challenge our faith beyond its current boundaries. He is the perfect teacher. Fully versed in His subject and fully aware of His student.

He loves His subject matter. Have you ever had a teacher who just loved the material they were teaching? Did that enthusiasm infect you? Did you come to love the subject also? And then to pursue it further than you thought you might? Jesus loves prayer. When He teaches you to pray, He will be teaching you His own heart. He will communicate His own joy to you and His joy will be in you and your joy will be full (John 15:11).

My sister Julie is a teacher. I don't mean that is her job. I mean that is who she is. She loves the subject she teaches and wants her students to love it. So, to that end, she is endlessly creative in how she will present the information so that it matters to them and engages them. She has goals past seeing her students do well on tests. She wants to see them become lifelong learners. It's just in her DNA— this love of instilling knowledge. Jesus is that kind of teacher multiplied to infinity. His love for prayer will be infectious. He will creatively design modules for your learning that will engage you fully and will be designed with just your learning style and personality and experience in mind. He'll be your private tutor while also bringing you into prayer experiences within the community of believers.

LEARNING PRAYER

You have access to the perfect Teacher in Rabbi Jesus. What will it take to be the best student—disciple—you can be so that you can learn all that He wants to impart?

First, believe. Believe Him. Believe that He is available to you and loves you and longs for you to experience all of Him that you possibly can. Let your heart listen in on a small portion of His prayer for you:

> *I have made you known to them, and will continue to make*
> *you known in order that the love you have for me may be*
> *in them and that I myself may be in them.*
>
> —JOHN 17:26

What He says about His disciples includes you. You are His disciple. He says that He has already made the Father known to you. The only reason you have a relationship with Christ is because He has made the Father known to you. The only reason you want to learn how to pray is because He has made the Father known to you. Remember that He said, "Everything that I learned from my Father I have made known to you" (John 15:15). But, look further. He will continue to make the Father known. He will keep teaching you. He always has more to disclose to you and it delights Him to continue showing you more and more of the Father.

What is the purpose of showing you more of the Father? In order that the very same love Jesus experiences from the Father may be reproduced in us. He prays that we will love Him the way the Father loves Him and that He Himself will be in us. The more we know the Father, the more we love the Son. The more we love the Son, the more His presence in us is made real to us. As our understanding of spiritual truth deepens and matures, so will our love for Him and our experience of His love for us. This is the very core of a praying life—the flow of love between your heart and His. He prayed for you that you would experience this reality. He wants you to know the essence of prayer, and He has asked that for you.

Can you believe this unbelievable truth? That the Lord of lords so loves you that He has taken up residence in you and yearns to impart to you what He alone knows and He alone can teach? That He has arranged your salvation so that it includes His indwelling presence and that He can teach you from the inside things that are too deep for you to learn or search out on your own? Listen to this promise: "Call to me and I will answer you and tell you great and unsearchable things you do not know" (Jeremiah 33:3).

First, believe Him. Second, yield to Him. Let Him run the show. Trust that He knows how to accomplish in you and for you exactly what He has in mind, and that He has in mind only your good. Your advancement. Your peace.

You can only yield to one you trust. Otherwise, you have to be ready to take the reins yourself in case things go off course. You have to be watching for a wrong move. You have to be careful and protective of your own course in case someone tries to head you in the wrong direction. Can you fully yield to Him, knowing that Jesus loves you beyond reason, with an obsessive love that hovers over you and manages even the smallest moments of your life?

First, believe. Second, yield. Third, follow. The call to prayer is not a command, but an invitation. He is calling you to a journey. He is calling you to follow Him (Mark 1:17). The call is active and risky. The great surprise in a praying life is that you find your little life swept up into the great purposes of God. Prayer is not passive or sedentary. It will catch you up in the current of His activity, and you will never be the same. Risky becomes safe when it is in response to the leading of Jesus.

Are you ready?

Are you ready to ask Jesus to teach you to pray? Are you ready to join Him in the grand expedition into all truth? Are you ready to lay aside anything He shows you that is slowing you down? Are you ready to run the race full throttle? Have you reached that place the first disciples must have reached where you can ask Him to teach you to pray like He prays because you are like a deer panting in the desert? Like a traveler in a dry and thirsty land? Nothing will satisfy except everything heaven has available. You can't think of settling for less than what He says is possible. Are you ready to live synced to His heart? Then, ask Him. "Lord, teach me to pray."

CHAPTER 3

OUR FATHER

*L*et me recap. Jesus' disciples—those who observed Him up close in the many settings and various encounters of His days—recognized a direct correlation between Jesus' life of prayer and His life of power. In His daily life—His living-in-real-time, walking-around life—Jesus lived in a flow of God's power. He acted with an instinctual knowledge of what the Father was doing and what the Father willed. He lived connected to the Father's heart. He lived synced.

The disciples were asking Him to teach them the kind of prayer that produced power and the kind that synced His heart to the Father's so that the Father's will was His normal.

As a rabbi, Jesus' intention was to teach from His life and to reproduce Himself in His disciples, not just to impart knowledge and theory and theology. So, it was understood between them that the request, "Teach us to pray," meant, "Teach us to pray like You pray. We want to live synced to Your heart like we see You living synced to the Father's heart."

When Jesus began teaching them to pray, He was giving insight into His own life of prayer. When He starts with, "Pray like this," it is not a command but an invitation. An invitation to learn from Him and to join Him in His praying life. He was, and is, inviting all His disciples (including you and me) to experience the kingdom of God through prayer.

The words and the form of the prayer He taught were familiar. The phrasing echoes that of many Jewish prayers with which His disciples would be familiar. It was common for rabbis to teach prayers to their disciples. It was not the words of Jesus' prayer that made it revolutionary but the way He lived the prayer He prayed. He was not simply spouting correct words in their correct forms and hoping to have pleased God with His performance; rather, He was opening His life to the Father's heart and receiving heaven's resources into His life. His faith was being fueled and His desires were being aligned.

When He opened His prayer with the address, "our Father," it was familiar wording. John Lightfoot, in *A Commentary on the New Testament from the Talmud and Hebraica*, quotes a familiar Jewish prayer using this form of address:

> *"Our Father which art in heaven, deal so with us as thou hast promised by the prophets." And in another place this is thrice recited; "Whom have we whereon to rely, besides our Father which is in heaven?" "Blessed are ye, O Israelites; who cleanseth you? Your Father, who is in heaven." "Ye gave not to your Father, who is in heaven, but to me the priest."*

The idea of God as Father was not foreign to Jewish thinking. The Old Testament hints at His father-relationship with His people, but it lacked the intimacy that Jesus gave it. Rabbi Jesus' preferred name for God was Father—Abba. He brought the concept of God's fatherhood from the fringes of thought to make it the center. He did not raise eyebrows by opening a Model Prayer with "our Father," but He sent shockwaves when He made that form of address intimate and personal and took it outside the prayer and into the life.

One of the most surprising truths that Jesus revealed about God is that we can call Him our Father in a personal, intimate relationship rather than as a formal and arms-length way. This offended the religious leaders of Jesus' day.

> *In his defense Jesus said to them, "My Father is always at his work to this very day, and I too am working." For this reason they tried all the more to kill him; not only was he breaking the Sabbath, but he was even calling God his own Father, making himself equal with God.*
>
> —JOHN 5:17–18

When He taught His disciples to pray like He prayed, the first lesson was our Father. When "our Father" is the headline, then the requests that follow are all defined by the intimate, loving, safe relationship of a father to His child.

THE INTIMACY OF OUR

Much has been written about the inclusiveness of teaching *our* Father, and I agree that is significant. But I want to camp on another aspect of *our* first. Remember Jesus is teaching you and me to say "our Father." Who's included in the *our?* Jesus. Jesus is inviting us into His relationship with the Father. He's saying, "My Father and your Father. Our Father." He is bringing us into His circle. In John 20:17 He stated it this way: "I am ascending to my Father and your Father, to my God and your God.'"

When I first got married to Wayne, *our* was something of a new word in my vocabulary. By nature, I am a fairly self-contained, self-sufficient person, and *I* and *my* came more naturally to me than *we* and *our*. At first, it felt a little like an intrusion. Suddenly, nothing was mine. Everything was ours—his and mine in equal measure. I didn't have the only say or the unchallenged opinion. Gradually, though, I began to experience the upside. I wasn't in this alone. I didn't have the whole load. I didn't have the full responsibility. Then, I took it one step further. Where at first I had trouble thinking of things I considered mine as ours, or life decisions that had been mine alone to make were now our decisions, now I saw that what had been only his was now ours as well. I didn't lose anything, and I gained everything that belonged to him. *Our* became a word about gain and intimacy rather than loss and dependence. What's mine is his, and what's his is mine. Our.

"*Our* Father," Jesus says. Your Father and My Father. "All things belong to you, and you belong to Christ; and Christ belongs to God" (1 Corinthians 3:22–23 NASB). What's His is yours. He has opened heaven's coffers and made the riches and power of the spiritual realm available to us just as His first disciples saw heaven's resources available to Jesus as He walked out life on earth as a man.

Not only does the intimacy of *our* bring you into possession of His resources but it also brings you into the unique communion that is the experience of the Godhead. You are pulled in to the circle of love and fellowship that exists among the Father, Son, and Spirit.

Jesus says to the Father: "All I have is yours, and all you have is mine" (John 17:10). The intimacy of *our* is on display. Here, He is specifically referring to the people, the disciples, that the Father has given Him. That includes you and me, as He also references all future disciples who will come to Him. Later in the same prayer He prays that "they may be one as we are one" (v. 11). He is praying for our unity with each other and among ourselves, but that unity grows out of the unity we have with Jesus. Observe how He expanded on that prayer:

> *That all of them may be one, Father, just as you are in me and I am in you. May they also be in us so that the world may believe that you have sent me. I have given them the glory that you gave me, that they may be one as we are one — I in them and you in me — so that they may be brought to complete unity.*
>
> —JOHN 17:21–23

He used His unity with the Father—His synchronized heart and life—as the model, The Father is in Jesus and Jesus is in the Father. They are so synced that they live and think and act in tandem. Next He adds: "May they [that includes you and me] also be in us" (v. 21, author's words added). In other words, "Let Us bring them into Our circle of love—that love that is uniquely Ours for each other. Let the loving unity with You that has been only My experience up to now be theirs as well." Sync us.

Remember, you belong to Christ and Christ belongs to God, so all things are yours. Are you seeing this? Jesus is willing to exchange His *Mine* for *Our*. He is willing to bring you and me into His riches and His relationship with the Father. The Father loves you like He loves Jesus! Writers are not supposed to use exclamation points, but I had to. This thought requires it. Don't you think?

Look further into His prayer: "I have given them the glory that you gave me" (v. 22). This glory to which Jesus refers is a different version of the eternal glory that is His alone as God. It is different from this glory: "Father, glorify me in your presence with the glory I had with you before the world began" (17:5). He differentiates between the glory God gave Him on earth and the glory He has had eternally as His own. He laid aside His own eternal glory and walked out His years on earth in the glory given Him by God. That's the glory He has passed along to His disciples.

What was His earthly glory? His glory while on earth was to show forth the Father and to manifest the Father through His person and life. "I have brought you glory on earth by finishing the work you gave me to do. . . . I have given them the glory that you gave me, that they may be one as we are one " (vv. 4, 22). The same way Jesus lived so synced to the Father's heart that to see Him was to see the Father, so He invites us to the same glory. We glorify Him by revealing Him. We reveal Him by living synced.

Now observe how He expounds that thought:

> *I have given them the glory that you gave me, that they*
> *may be one as we are one—I in them and you in me—*
> *so that they may be brought to complete unity. Then the*

*world will know that you sent me and have loved them
even as* [in the same way; in the same measure] *you have
loved me.*

—JOHN 17:22–23 (author's words added)

Our lives synced to His puts us in the position of being loved by the
Father the way Jesus is loved by the Father. Very same way.

1 + 1 = 1

This unity to which Jesus is referring is not a unity among His disciples as such, but rather a unity among His disciples as a result of each
disciple's unity with Jesus and Jesus' unity with God. Because Jesus
is in us, we are one with each other. "I (Jesus) in them (you and me)
and You (Father) in Me (Jesus)." We become recipient and also dis-
penser of the love that is the ground zero of all love, the love of which
all other forms of love are but shadows, the love that is unflinching
and unremitting and unabashed and unrestrained. Lavish love. Jesus
prayed "that the love you have for me may be in them and that I
myself may be in them" (John 17:26). His *Mine* has become *Our*. An
unfathomable honor has been bestowed on us.

"But whoever is united with the Lord is one with him in spirit"
(1 Corinthians 6:17). We can live so synced to the heart of Jesus that
we are one with Him the same way that He is one with the Father.
"Anyone who has seen me has seen the Father. How can you say,
'Show us the Father'? Don't you believe that I am in the Father, and
that the Father is in me? . . . On that day [i.e., when the Holy Spirit
has come to indwell you and reveal all truth] you will realize that

I am in my Father, and you are in me, and I am in you" (John 14:9–10; 20, author's words added). This being synced to Him is so beyond human reasoning or human intellect's ability to grasp that it will require the Holy Spirit Himself to reveal it and make it real to us.

The new math in the new kingdom goes like this: The One + this one = One. Jesus (the One) and me (this one) living connected so that we are living in tandem. This is the equation for living synced.

JESUS THE FIRSTBORN

And we know that in all things God works for the good of those who love him, who have been called according to his purpose. For those God foreknew he also predestined to be conformed to the image of his Son, that he might be the firstborn among many brothers and sisters.

—ROMANS 8:28–29

Jesus has brought us into His family. We share a Father with Him. He, the only begotten, and we, the adopted, grafted-in ones. That adoption gives us full stature as children of the Father and brothers and sisters of the Firstborn. He has made it possible for us to be born again of His Spirit and brought into His family.

Jewish definition of firstborn is "opener of the womb." Until there is a firstborn there can be no subsequent births. The firstborn opens the way for his siblings to be born and is considered the first-fruit of the womb. The firstfruit belonged to God—whether sons, animals, or crops—and in offering the firstfruit to Him, the offerer expressed faith that this was the first of much to follow.

All Jewish firstborn sons were required to be redeemed at 30 days in a prescribed ceremony known as *pidyon haben*—redeeming the firstborn. This is what Mary and Joseph were doing at the temple when Simeon saw the infant Jesus and recognized Him as Messiah (Luke 2:22–32).

> *When the time came for the purification rites required by the Law of Moses, Joseph and Mary took him to Jerusalem to present him to the Lord (as it is written in the Law of the Lord, "Every firstborn male is to be consecrated to the Lord"), and to offer a sacrifice in keeping with what is said in the Law of the Lord: "a pair of doves or two young pigeons."*
>
> —LUKE 2:22–24

At its first institution, this was directly related to the Exodus from Egypt.

> *The LORD said to Moses, "Consecrate to me every first-born male. The first offspring of every womb among the Israelites belongs to me, whether human or animal." Then Moses said to the people, "Redeem every firstborn among your sons. In days to come, when your son asks you, 'What does this mean?' say to him, 'With a mighty hand the LORD brought us out of Egypt, out of the land of slavery. When Pharaoh stubbornly refused to let us go, the LORD killed the firstborn of both people and animals in Egypt. This is why I sacrifice to the LORD the first male offspring of every womb and redeem each of my firstborn sons.' And it will be like*

a sign on your hand and a symbol on your forehead that
the LORD brought us out of Egypt with his mighty hand."

—EXODUS 13:1–3, 13–16

On the night of the tenth plague in Egypt, God claimed every first-born son. Only firstborn sons under the blood were spared. The first-born son was a living testament to the redemption of the Israelites from Egypt and slavery into the Promised Land and freedom.

The firstborn held a particular place in Jewish thinking and as firstborn, was the beginning of a line. Jesus, our firstborn Brother, opened the way for us to be born again by the Spirit.

> *He came to that which was his own, but his own did not*
> *receive him. Yet to all who did receive him, to those who*
> *believed in his name, he gave the right to become chil-*
> *dren of God—children born not of natural descent, nor of*
> *human decision or a husband's will, but born of God.*
>
> —JOHN 1:11–13

Jesus, our Brother, is a living testament of God's loving redemption, and He has paid the redemption price in full to lead His band of brothers and sisters out of bondage. He has joined Himself to us and is not ashamed to call us His brothers and sisters.

> *Both the one who makes people holy and those who are*
> *made holy are of the same family. So Jesus is not ashamed*
> *to call them brothers and sisters. He says, "I will declare*
> *your name to my brothers and sisters; in the assembly*

I will sing your praises." And again, "I will put my trust
in him." And again he says, "Here am I, and the chil-
dren God has given me." Since the children have flesh and
blood, he too shared in their humanity so that by his death
he might break the power of him who holds the power of
death—that is, the devil—and free those who all their lives
were held in slavery by their fear of death.

—HEBREWS 2:11–15

He is so identified with us that He was willing to take on flesh and
blood to participate in our humanity. He shared in our nature so that
we could share in His. "For by these He has granted to us His precious
and magnificent promises, so that by them you may become partakers
of *the* divine nature, having escaped the corruption that is in the world
by lust" (2 Peter 1:4 NASB). He came down to us so that He could
lift us into His realm. "And God raised us up with Christ and seated
us with him in the heavenly realms in Christ Jesus" (Ephesians 2:6).

When Jesus invites us to open prayer with *Our* Father, remember that this is not a throwaway phrase. It is costly and precious. It
is a privilege bought with a high price. It speaks of the intimacy that
the Father and the Son long to have with you and were willing to do
whatever it would take to achieve. An intimacy so complete that you
and I can live synced to the heart of Jesus.

OUR LIVED OUT

Knowing this to be fundamental and primal in Jesus praying, how did
it look in His living? First, we see that His actions and ministry were

driven by compassion. "When he saw the crowds, he had compassion on them, because they were harassed and helpless, like sheep without a shepherd" (Matthew 9:36). Compassion means to feel deeply with. Compassion implies to feel the same feelings as another, not just to feel sorry for another. Compassion means that your identification with another is so deep that you feel what another is feeling.

To really have compassion for others, you will need to have walked a similar road. You feel their feelings because you have felt those feelings yourself somewhere along the way. Jesus took on flesh and blood and identified completely with us. He has compassion on us. "For we do not have a high priest who is unable to empathize with our weaknesses, but we have one who has been tempted in every way, just as we are—yet he did not sin" (Hebrews 4:15).

But feeling with us is not the end of Jesus' compassion toward us. His compassion compels Him to act on our behalf. Where you see Jesus' compassion aroused, you see action taken.

The story of Lazarus and his sisters gives a glimpse into how Jesus' compassion goes into action (John 11:1–46). In this story, we see Jesus crying unashamedly in public in front of everyone gathered. He is deeply moved by the plight and the heartbreak of His dear friends Mary and Martha. Their brother, Lazarus, had been dead for four days and they were grieving. Jesus knew and had known since the beginning that He would raise Lazarus from the dead. He knew their grief would be short-lived and would quickly turn to rejoicing. Yet, He cried. He felt their grief and pain as His own.

When my children were little, and would experience hurts or disappointments, I would feel their pain deeply. Even though I had an adult's perspective and knew that the momentary hurt would soon fade and be forgotten, I felt the pain of their moment. I think that is what Jesus is experiencing in the Lazarus story. That is how great His love and His connection with them reaches. Though He knows their pain is fleeting, He feels their pain as they walk through their circumstance.

However, Jesus' compassion does not end with feeling pain with us. His compassion moves Him to action. He raises Lazarus from the dead, feeds the hungry crowds, heals the sick, and delivers the demon-possessed. He is moved by compassion.

Over and over we see Him wading into the very messiest lives and situations because His compassion—His identity with us—is so complete that He cannot see us in pain without feeling pain Himself. He doesn't work things out for us from a distance. Instead, He puts Himself right into the muck and the mire of our lives and walks with us while He works on our behalf. He comforts and sustains while He releases His power and provision for our benefit. He's in it with us and for us. You can be assured that any pain we walk through is necessary to the greater good He is working out on our behalf. He saves us all the hurt and heartache He can without compromising what He is producing in our lives.

During His earthly walk, how did Jesus find those who needed His compassionate touch? They just showed up as He lived out His day. He was synced to the Father's heart and so found Himself in the right place at the right time. He didn't have to seek them out. They crossed His path, seemingly randomly. What looked like chance was carefully orchestrated by the Father. He walked in the "good works, which God prepared in advance for [Him] to do" (Ephesians 2:10, author's words added). He did not have to strain and seek for the assignments of compassion the Father had for Him on any given day. They simply appeared.

I described some of these encounters in my book *Set Apart* like this:

MERCY IN MOTION

THE LIFE GIVER

As the leper struggled through the crowd, his bell announced his shame. "Unclean. Unclean." All the clean ones moved away, avoiding his pain at all costs. The leper worked his way through the religious throng, desperate to find the presence of Jesus.

Jesus looked past his rotting flesh and saw the hope that sloughed away with every rejection, every head that turned away, every face that registered disgust and fear.

Jesus looked past the stench of decaying skin and saw the little spark of life crusted over with loneliness and hurt, almost extinguished.

He heard the anguished cry: "If you are willing, you can make me clean." He restored the leper's disease-ravaged body, but more than that, He restored his shame-ravaged soul. The fearless, compassionate touch of the Savior clothed the man in dignity. Jesus gave him more than a reprieve from death. Jesus gave him life. (See Matthew 8:1–3.)

The Restorer

They hauled her through the streets, her guilt on display for all to see. No place for her to hide, no shelter from accusing glances and condemning words. She was a perfect target for their collective righteous outrage. A perfect target for the stones they itched to throw.

They dragged her into the presence of Jesus. Just how far would He carry His theme of mercy and compassion? Surely this woman would find mercy's limits. Surely He would have no choice but to join them in their stone-throwing censure.

In Jesus' presence, the stone-throwers discovered that His compassion never fails, His mercies never come to an end. He unmasked the surface righteousness of her accusers and set her free—forgiven. (See John 8:2–11.)

The Heart Cleanser

He was so close, and yet He might as well have been a world away. To reach the presence of Jesus, she would have to wade through the conglomerate of very, very religious ones—the perfectly righteous men—who were His dinner companions today. She would drown in their scorn. Surely she could not keep her head above the waves of their belittling hatred, which were sure to swallow her up. So close! So close!

The longing could not be contained. She had seen the mercy in His eyes when they fell on her that day. He didn't say a word. No one knew but her. When she read the forgiveness in His face, saw the mercy in His glance, she had been born again. A clean slate. A fresh start. A heart flushed out and free of sin's debris. Healed from wounds that festered in her soul. New.

Whatever it took, she would bring Him her most precious possession. She would break it at His feet and pour out everything she owned as her worship and adoration. She would wash His feet with her tears, as He had washed her heart with His mercy.

Breaking through the rigid righteousness of the religious, she found the gentle mercy of the Savior. At Jesus' feet, she who had come to lower herself in His presence, found herself lifted up in the presence of her enemies. She left that day, clean. (See Luke 7:36–50.)

When we are living synced to His heart, the pain of others will move us. We will not be able to stay aloof and unmoved by others' situations. His love is poured into our hearts so that His love flows from us to others (Romans 5:5). Jesus prayed "that the love you have for me may be in them and that I myself may be in them" (John 17:26). Did you catch that? The very same love that the Father has toward the Son will be in us.

When we are living synced, those whom God has appointed to receive compassion from us will show up in our way, on our way. Just living our daily lives will bring us into contact with those whom the Father wants to love through us.

LIVING SYNCED: WHO KNEW
A HAT COULD SAVE A LIFE?

Author Lucinda Secrest McDowell tells this story of how a synced life looks:

Today my friend who has a ministry in the inner city gave me a warm winter hat. One of many lovingly made by God's people to hand out to the cold who have no warmth. This blue fleece cap was an extra after hundreds of toys and clothes had been distributed during the holiday season. In sharing this, Vicki told an incredible story.

And it all began about a week ago when she had taken a hungry child through McDonald's in Hartford in order to treat her to some chicken nuggets.

As the window attendant handed her the order, Vicki graciously offered her one of the new warm winter hats, wished her a Merry Christmas and drove away. Responding to promptings of the Holy Spirit comes naturally to this woman who has been a minister to children and families for more than a quarter century. She knew that sewn inside each hat was a tag saying "God Loves You. Camp Hope." Or "Peace. Hope. Love. God Bless You."

But she never suspected that giving one hat could literally save a life.

This week Vicki was stunned to receive a message forwarded from the folks at Camp Hope (where many of these hats were made by people who wanted to donate them to the needy). Turns out, it was written by the window attendant from that McDonald's order.

"Hello, my name is _____.

Today I received a winter hat working in the McDonald's drive thru by a lady whom I wish I had asked her name. On the inside of the hat it said "God loves you. Camp Hope." And I hope I'm writing to the right place.

If I am and if you happen to know who this woman is, I'd like to thank her. I've been a Christian since age 15 and I've always been strong in my faith even with my share of trials. But for the past year or so I've suffered from major anxiety and depression. This morning I woke up with the intention of not living another day. My boss called this morning saying he needed me early so I decided I was gonna do it (kill myself) after work.

It is true that God comes at the right time. Seeing that message at that moment served as a reminder that I am loved. And not just by anyone but by God, creator of *everything*! Sometimes we forget about something so amazing as that.

One thing I've realized that as humans we don't question God's ability to do things but his willingness to do things for us, because we fail daily and don't think He'd do things for us. We just have to keep faith that God does love us and is willing to do anything for us.

In summation, I just want to thank her for letting God use her in such a way that seems small, but for me it was great. God used her to save my life.

Well, if you do know who this woman might be if you can kindly show her this message. If not, well it was worth a try. Maybe this testimony can be of blessing.

Best, _____"

A hat. A giver. An intentional act.

All working together to be the answer to a prayer for hope—for life out of death.

THE FATHER

Jesus invites us into His intimacy with His Father and opens the door for us to call *His* Father *our* Father. I want to change emphasis now and focus on what it really means that God is our Father, Daddy, Papa.

As Jesus lived synced to the Father's heart, He lived with His soul at peace. He lived in a state of soul rest. What did He say we would find when we learn from Him? What one, single attribute did He say would be ours when we accepted His invitation to learn from Him? You will find rest for your souls. Why will rest be our take away? Because as our Rabbi reproduces Himself in us, His central characteristic will become evident in us. Who He is shapes who we are. He considers a restful soul to be the definition of His demeanor. It is what He offers us, as if He considers it worth the cost of following Him.

LIVING AT REST

Rest for your soul. Let the words wrap themselves around your heart. Rest for your soul. Let the promise flow into your mind and take up residence there. Rest for your soul.

Learn from Jesus. As you learn more and more about who He is, you will find anxiety losing its hold on you; you will find bitterness, anger, and defensiveness retreating; you will find uncertainty and fear yielding to boldness and stoutheartedness. In Him is an unending soul rest.

He modeled soul rest. What a rabbi offered was not simply what he knew, but who he was. Essentially, Jesus is standing before the crowds saying, "Look at Me. Observe Me. Do you want to experience what you see Me experiencing? You can have this peace and confidence—this rest. Follow Me and this is what you will learn."

Where did Jesus learn this rest? From His Father. The Father lives in a state of Sabbath rest, and Jesus lived synced to the Father's heart so the Father's restful state was downloaded into the heart of the Son.

What does the Word say about the restful state in which the Father lives? We begin to see it in the concept of Sabbath. Sabbath is more than a day of the week. It is a state of the soul. It describes the state in which God perpetually lives and invites us to live with Him at peace, at rest.

The first mention of Sabbath is in Genesis 2:2–3:

> By the seventh day God had finished the work he had been doing; so on the seventh day he rested from all his work. Then God blessed the seventh day and made it holy, because on it he rested from all the work of creating that he had done.

Notice the tie-in created by the word *so*. God had finished His work, *so* He rested. Why did God rest? Had He exhausted Himself? The Scripture is clear: God rested because He was finished. He was finished with all of His work, so He Sabbathed. He ceased. The word *Sabbath* means "to be finished; to have completed the work." It doesn't mean just taking a break or resting until one recovers. It means to be finished.

God created for six days, and then He Sabbathed. For how long did He Sabbath? Did He pick up where He'd left off when day eight dawned? God, on the seventh day of creation, began a Sabbath that was to last forever. "And yet his works have been finished since the creation of the world" (Hebrews 4:3).

God's work has been in a finished state, completed, since day seven. When was the Lamb slain? Before the world began (Revelation 13:8). When were the names of those who would be saved written in the book of life? Before the world began (Revelation 17:8; Ephesians 1:4). When was the kingdom prepared for believers? Before the world began (Matthew 25:34). Look at 2 Thessalonians 2:13; 2 Timothy 1:9; Titus 1:1–2; and Ephesians 2:10.

All of His work was finished, and so He Sabbathed.

Yet Jesus stated, "My Father is always at his work to this very day, and I too am working" (John 5:17). At one level, everything is finished. God's work in its finished state is on the spiritual realm. The work left to do is to release it into the material realm in the fullness of time.

> *This grace was given us in Christ Jesus before the beginning of time, but it has now been revealed through the*

appearing of our Savior, Christ Jesus, who has destroyed death and has brought life and immortality to light through the gospel.

—2 TIMOTHY 1:9–10

Do you see what this means? The action—grace was given us in Christ Jesus—was completed before the beginning of time. But God revealed it in Christ's coming to earth. God's work is finished, but it will be revealed on the earth at its ripe and appointed moment.

Jesus lived with His soul in a Sabbath because His Father lives in a Sabbath. Jesus knew that no matter what came His way, the Father had finished the work related to it and would reveal that finished work in the right way at the right time.

Sabbath for you and me means living our lives in absolute surrender and total trust in the finished work of Christ. Not only is the salvation work finished in Him but every need that comes into our lives has already been provided for, every dilemma has already been resolved, every question has already been answered. We simply have to place our lives in the flow of His provision. Simply abide in Christ. Simply live where the power is operating. Hear Him say, "Come to Me. You will find rest for your soul."

Jesus lived out His life on earth with His soul at rest because He knew His Father had covered all the bases. All He had to do in times that might have caused fear and stress was to sync His heart to the Father's. Jesus walked naturally in the flow of His Father's peace. We'll look at some evidence that He had to battle to a place of peace sometimes. But once there, He walked in it and it emanated from Him as His natural state.

LIKE FATHER, LIKE SON

No one has ever seen God, but the one and only Son, who is himself God and is in closest relationship with the Father, has made him known.

—JOHN 1:18

If you really know me, you will know my Father as well. From now on, you do know him and have seen him.

—JOHN 14:7

Anyone who has seen me has seen the Father.

—JOHN 14:9

The one who looks at me is seeing the one who sent me.

—JOHN 12:45

Since His Father lives in a state of Sabbath, at rest, in peace, the Son also lived in peace. In the Gospel accounts, we see Jesus living in chaotic situations with life roiling around Him, but His heart is at rest. His bearing is calm and kind and patient. Unruffled in conflict, steady in unexpected situations, gentle with the broken, kind to the harsh. His peace comes from knowing that He is in the Father's care. That every moment is fully supplied by His loving Father.

The relationship is Father to Son—rather than, say, king to sub-ject or master to slave. A father has a whole different kind of love toward his child than does a king to his subject or a master to his slave. A father dotes on his child, works and plans for his child's benefit, provides for his child. Everything a father has is available to his child. In the other relationships, the subservient one is valued for what that one can add to the master. In the father to child relationship, the father is seeking to add to his child. Everything the father plans or supplies is to benefit his child. Living synced, Jesus lived fully aware of His Father's love. This reality produced calm in His emotions and confidence in His actions. He promised His disciples that they could live in His love just the same way they had seen Him live in His Father's love (John 15:9–10). To offer them this love as a promised benefit, Jesus had to have known that, indeed, His experience of the Father's love was observable and desirable.

Jesus knows His Father's heart toward Him because He kept His heart attuned to the Father's. He kept the eyes of His heart glued to the Father's face. He kept His mind stayed on the Father's words. He was steady and sure because He knew the Father and let the Father reproduce Himself in the Son. He could hold Himself up as a living mirror, perfectly reflecting the Father. He seemed to be saying in essence, "Do you see peace ruling My life? Then you see the Father's peace reproduced in Me."

"You will keep in perfect peace those whose minds are steadfast, because they trust in you" (Isaiah 26:3).

The Hebrew word translated "perfect peace," and the word that defined peace for Jesus, is *shalom*. It means more than absence of conflict. It means being fully supplied and provided for. This is very likely the word Jesus used when He promised "rest for your soul." At the very least, it was the idea He was communicating. The Hebrew word translated "steadfast" has the sense of being fixed and immoveable. A person whose heart and mind are anchored to the Father's will be in the Father's keeping, fully supplied and provided for.

> *They will have no fear of bad news; their hearts are stead-fast, trusting in the LORD. Their hearts are secure, they will have no fear; in the end they will look in triumph on their foes.*
>
> —PSALM 112:7–8

This psalm is describing the person whose heart is steadfastly fixed on the Lord, fully trusting in Him. A person who is living synced. That person need not fear bad news. Think about bad news. Often, it comes out of nowhere and blindsides us. Often, it is not something we have prepared for. It takes us by surprise. But we don't have to fear that kind of news because our Father has prepared for it, and He is not surprised.

We have a tendency to fear bad news, even when there is no bad news. We fear that bad news might be just around the corner. We worry that bad news is coming and that very fear robs us of living in the moment. We expend emotion needlessly by worrying that bad news is coming.

Jesus did not live in fear of bad news. He knew that whatever came, He would be fully supplied by His Father. He did not feel compelled to worry ahead because He knew that whatever bad news He might encounter, He would find the Father's provision in place. This peace and confidence did not come from the idea that nothing bad would ever happen, but rather that anything bad or difficult would be under the careful supervision of His Father.

William Garden Blaikie in *Glimpses of the Inner Life of Christ* says:

> Through life, therefore, He had the calm and pleasant
> feeling that nothing could happen to Him that was not
> in harmony with that will which was infinitely holy and
> wise and good. Things might happen which were deeply
> painful, but nothing could happen that was not right. Of
> some things that were essential to the work which He had
> undertaken, the pain might be excessive; but even that was
> all under the control of the Father, and would eventually
> work for good.

This soul rest Jesus offers to those of us who choose to follow Him
was fleshed out by Him in the days of His incarnation. As He lived
His life depending on the provision of His Father, the result was that
He lived in perfect peace.

LIVING SYNCED: THE HOUSE
THAT PRAYER BUILT

George Mueller was a man who lived synced to the Father's heart.
A hallmark of his life was peace in the midst of challenges to his faith
as he was determined to let God make all provision for the orphan-
ages he established. Arthur T. Pierson writes in *George Müller of
Bristol and His Witness to a Prayer-Hearing God*:

> Every day brought new demands for continuance in
> prayer. In fact, as Mr. Müller testifies, the only difference

between latter and former days was that the difficulties were greater in proportion as the work was larger. But he adds that this was to be expected, for the Lord gives faith for the very purpose of trying it for the glory of His own name and the good of him who has the faith, and it is by these very trials that trust learns the secret of its triumphs.

Ed Reese in *The Life and Ministry of George Mueller* recounts this story:

One morning the plates and cups and bowls on the table were empty. There was no food in the larder, and no money to buy food. The children were standing waiting for their morning meal, when Mueller said, "Children, you know we must be in time for school." Lifting his hand he said, "Dear Father, we thank Thee for what Thou art going to give us to eat." There was a knock on the door. The baker stood there, and said, "Mr. Mueller, I couldn't sleep last night. Somehow I felt you didn't have bread for breakfast and the Lord wanted me to send you some. So I got up at 2 a.m. and baked some fresh bread, and have brought it."

Mueller thanked the man. No sooner had this transpired when there was a second knock at the door. It was the milkman. He announced that his milk cart had broken down right in front of the Orphanage, and he would like to give the children his cans of fresh milk so he could empty his wagon and repair it. No wonder, years later, when Mueller was to travel the world as an evangelist, he would be heralded as "the man who gets things from God!"

THE BATTLE FOR PEACE

In the fourth chapter of Hebrews, the writer reminds his audience that God offers rest to His people. This is the passage where we read that God has been in a Sabbath rest since the seventh day of creation because His work is finished (v. 3). He invites His people to join Him in that soul rest. Then the writer makes this odd statement, exhorting us to "make every effort [strive, work hard, be determined] to enter that rest" (v. 11, author's words added). Doesn't that seem incongruous? Work hard to rest?

Look at Jesus, who—as we have been saying—lived at rest. We noted that His peaceful, unruffled, steady, poised deportment seemed to be a hallmark of His life. So much so that this is what He promised to reproduce in His disciples when they chose to follow Him. Let's look to His example to see what it looks like to make every effort to be at rest.

If you and I are continually assaulted with circumstances and emotions that threaten to steal our peace, then imagine the assault on the Son of God. The enemy pursued Him relentlessly, I'm sure seeking to introduce doubt, fear, and worry. He felt deeply for the sorrows of those He came to save and their pain pained Him. He was far more tuned in to the struggles of others than you and I could ever be. He was surrounded by threats to His own person, insults from high-profile leaders, and rejection from those He loved. Yet He walked out His days with His soul at rest. What was His secret?

What was the key to His peace that He promised to pass on to His followers?

His secret was that He knew Almighty God as His Father. He knew where to take His burdens and His fears. He knew how to sync His troubled heart to the Father's peaceful heart until the peace that surpasses knowledge and understanding flushed out any concern, until His soul found its resting place in the sovereign power and unrelenting love of His Father. He knew how to make every effort to enter God's rest. Later, we'll look at situations in which prayer became His battle ground—the place where He battled His natural human emotions into submission to the faith that brought peace and tranquility.

Look with me at this moment when Jesus' heart was troubled.

> *The hour has come for the Son of Man to be glorified. Very truly I tell you, unless a kernel of wheat falls to the ground and dies, it remains only a single seed. But if it dies, it produces many seeds. Anyone who loves their life will lose it, while anyone who hates their life in this world will keep it for eternal life. Whoever serves me must follow me; and where I am, my servant also will be. My Father will honor the one who serves me. Now my soul is troubled, and what shall I say? "Father, save me from this hour"? No, it was for this very reason I came to this hour. Father, glorify your name!*
>
> —JOHN 12:23–28

I find this passage fascinating because it is almost like we are listening in as Jesus processes His fear and reaches faith. We get a master class in the battleground of prayer, moving fear to faith and worry to worship.

The crucifixion looms. The hour has come. His soul is troubled—agitated, stirred up, in agony. I think He says aloud what He has been working through in His private hours with the Father. He is teaching His disciples, but also solidifying for Himself.

> *Unless a kernel of wheat falls to the ground and dies, it remains only a single seed. But if it dies, it produces many seeds. Anyone who loves their life will lose it, while anyone who hates their life in this world will keep it for eternal life.*
>
> —JOHN 12:24–25

He's letting this truth put down roots. He will endure the Cross because what that horror will produce will outweigh the agony.

Then He states it outright. "My soul is troubled" (v. 27). He lets us in on His thoughts and struggles. "What shall I say? 'Father, save me from this hour'?" Because that is what He wants to say. The humanity in Him—the natural inclination of His human nature—wants to say that. He's already battled it out in prayer. Conclusion? He is reminded of His purpose. I feel sure the Father gently and firmly reminded Him that this is what it will take to win our freedom—the freedom of those He has come to so fully identify with. This is it. And then, the victory. "*Father*, glorify your name" (v. 28, author's emphasis).

His struggle was put to rest as He subjugated His emotions to the purpose of the Father.

Beyond the emotion was the will. At His core, He willed the Father to glorify His name, and His emotions did not rule His actions. And the outcome? My son Stinson puts it this way:

> Really hit home today that the Cross was nothing more than a torture device. Used to torture, humiliate, and intimidate. But, through Christ, it became a symbol of power and hope to the very same people in whom it was supposed to instill fear. Torture is a deplorable method used to break someone's spirit. Christ was tortured to death but used the enemy's best fear tactic as a catalyst and as a podium to usher the Holy Spirit into our hearts.

MAGNIFIED

Jesus brought the Father into clear focus. He magnified the Lord. When you put something invisible to the naked eye on a slide and put it under a microscope, the invisible becomes visible. Not only is it visible, but it is magnified so that the details are clear and discernable. What was hidden is revealed. This is what Jesus did in His earthly form. "No one has ever seen God, the one and only Son, who is himself God and is the closest relationship with the Father, has made him known" (John 1:18).

Jesus showed us the Father. He brought out the details and put the Father on display for all to see. The fact that God is your Father is not just a lovely idea or a comforting thought. It has day-by-day, minute-by-minute practical effect in your life. He is your provider. He's going to take care of you. He knows what you need and has already made arrangements to provide it. Like Jesus, you can live with your soul in a Sabbath. You can walk in His provision, synced to His heart.

Because God is your Father, rather than just your caretaker, He delights in meeting your needs and fulfilling your desires. His activity in your life is not restricted to the minimum of making sure your basic needs are met. He goes beyond that. As your Father, He loves your joy.

When my boys were young, they loved amusement parks. I loved to take them to amusement parks. Why did I love that? Not because I loved the rides. I fear heights and dislike spinning around. Not because I loved the crowds. I feel claustrophobic in loud, crowded places. Not because I enjoyed the heat. I avoid being hot and sweaty as much as possible. So, nearly everything about the experience is something I dislike, but I loved taking my boys to amusement parks. Why? What brought me pleasure? I loved their joy.

Your Father loves your joy. It delights Him to delight you. Little things. Unexpected experiences. Small evidences of His attention to the details of your life. He loves that.

LIVING SYNCED: THE WOMAN IN THE MIRROR

Authors Bill and Pam Farrel tell a classic story from their honeymoon that has become a defining moment in their relationship. It goes something like this: As Pam was looking in a mirror, putting on makeup, she began to list all her perceived imperfections. Bill stopped her and said, "From now on, I'll be your mirror." They relayed that story during an interview on Focus on the Family's radio show, and singer-songwriter Rebecca Friedlander was listening. She was taken by the story, and said to herself, "That's how we should see Jesus. He should be our mirror." She hadn't caught the names of the couple she heard, but the saying had burrowed into her heart and made itself at home. She wrote a song based on the thought, and couldn't imagine how one day she could meet the couple who had so touched her with their story.

The song aired, had international Christian TV airplay, was featured in the Christian film *Girl Perfect*, and became one of Rebecca's most popular songs.

After traveling to Alaska to make a music video for the song she titled "Mirror," Rebecca posted the song on her friend, Debbie Douglass's, Facebook page because the two had collaborated on some photo shoots while in Alaska.

While traveling, Pam jumped on to social media to check in and watched a beautiful inspiring video called "Mirror" that was posted on her friend Debbie's page. So moved by the kindred message from her honeymoon, she shot a message to the young songwriter praising the video and gave a hint that she, too, had a "Mirror" story. Rebecca messaged back that if Pam had a moment, she would love to talk by phone. Within a few sentences, Rebecca shared how the song had been inspired by a couple she heard on Focus on the Family. Pam exclaimed with joy, "That was me! That was my husband Bill who said those words of love to me more than 35 years ago!"

Rebecca says,

> I didn't remember the name of the couple on Focus, but I remembered the sound of Pam's voice. In the few

minutes, between chatting on Facebook and receiving Pam's call, it dawned on me that she could have been the one to inspire it, and I jumped online to do some research. When I heard her voice on the phone, I was 99 percent sure it was her, and started shaking with Holy Spirit excitement! It was the most beautiful moment to be able to thank her for her ministry in the kingdom and say, 'God is using your ministry in ways you have no idea of! Your message has reached people in ways you don't even know about!' I was so honored to be able to say thank you! When I met Pam, I was able to tell her that the song she inspired had been shared around the world and touched people, including the young generation!

In an instant, a kindred friendship formed. Soon after, Rebecca came to Pam and Bill's to record a video of the story to be featured along with the stories of women around the world whose lives had also been transformed when they grasped their beauty from a more heavenly point of view and welcomed Jesus to be their "Mirror."

CHAPTER 5

THE HEAVENS

"Our Father in heaven," Jesus taught us to pray. The word translated "heaven" is plural, so *our Father in the heavens* is the sense. Why does that matter? We tend to think of heaven as a land far away where we will go when we die. Something reserved for our future with little relevance to our present. I think when we see how Jesus thought of heaven—interacting daily with heaven's resources—we will get a new view of this wonderful phrase.

Scripture uses the phrase "the heavens" in several ways, the meaning made clear by its context. Occasionally, it refers to the heavenly bodies in the sky that were formed at creation.

> *In the beginning God created the heavens and the earth.*
>
> —GENESIS 1:1

> *The heavens declare the glory of God; the skies proclaim the work of his hands.*
>
> —PSALM 19:1

Occasionally, it refers to our eternal home.

> *For we know that if the earthly tent we live in is destroyed,*
> *we have a building from God, an eternal house in heaven,*
> *not built by human hands.*
>
> —2 CORINTHIANS 5:1

Sometimes, it refers to the exclusive abode of God the Father, God the Son, God the Spirit, and His angels where He sits on His eternal throne.

> *Heaven is my throne, and the earth is my footstool.*
>
> —ACTS 7:49

Most often, the heavenly realms are considered part of our present reality, accessible to us right now. The spiritual realm is real and active and present but invisible. The spiritual realm with which we interact regularly is the aspect of reality where God's power and provision are in effect and our praying lives are moving heaven's resources into the circumstances of earth. If we could see the spiritual realm with our physical eyes, we would see constant activity. We would see angels sent to minister to believers, warfare between Satan's realm and the armies of God, and provision available for our circumstances.

Explore briefly what Scripture teaches about the present interaction between the material realm (earth) and the spiritual realm (heaven):

> *Praise be to the God and Father of our Lord Jesus Christ,*

who has blessed us in the heavenly realms with every spiritual blessing in Christ.

—EPHESIANS 1:3

He [God] exerted when he raised Christ from the dead and seated him at his right hand in the heavenly realms.

—EPHESIANS 1:20 (author's words added)

God raised us up with Christ and seated us with him in the heavenly realms in Christ Jesus.

—EPHESIANS 2:6

His intent was that now, through the church, the manifold wisdom of God should be made known to the rulers and authorities in the heavenly realms.

—EPHESIANS 3:10

For our struggle is not against flesh and blood, but against the rulers, against the authorities, against the powers of this dark world and against the spiritual forces of evil in the heavenly realms.

—EPHESIANS 6:12

Since, then, you have been raised with Christ, set your hearts on things above, where Christ is, seated at the right hand of God. Set your minds on things above, not on earthly things. For you died, and your life is now hidden with Christ in God.

—COLOSSIANS 3:1–3

HEAVEN'S POWER FOR EARTH'S CIRCUMSTANCES

The spiritual realm is as much part of our daily living as the material realm. Because of the indwelling, present Jesus, we have immediate and direct access to the spiritual realm and all the power and provision it holds. Jesus is the open door from earth to heaven.

Notice how interconnected the material realm and the spiritual realm are.

Jesus is in the spiritual realm. God has "seated him at his right hand in the heavenly realms" (Ephesians 1:20). Yet, *Jesus is in us.* He describes the union this way: "I [Jesus] in them [you and me] and you [Father] in me [Jesus]" (John 17:23, author's words added). Paul says, "Christ lives in me" (Galatians 2:20). Author Max Lucado summarizes it this way: "The mystery of Christianity is summarized in *Colossians 1:27*, '*Christ is in you!*' The Christian is a person in whom Christ is happening!"

I live on earth, yet I am in Christ (1 Corinthians 1:30; Romans 8:1). My life is hidden in Christ (Colossians 3:3). Earth is the material realm and Christ is in the spiritual realm. "God raised us up with Christ and seated us with him in the heavenly realms in Christ Jesus" (Ephesians 2:6).

Scripture presents both realities as equally true at the same time: on earth and in heaven. Jesus is where heaven and earth meet. He became a man, and as a man, was powered by the Spirit and led by the Father. He lived in the environment of earth by the power of heaven. When He comes to make His home in you (John 14:23), He is the convergence of heaven and earth.

In the Gospels, we see Jesus as He lived His life on earth in the power of heaven—synced. While on earth, He limited Himself to His humanity and lived that humanity empowered by the Spirit. When He lived out His human nature by the Spirit's power and the Father's leading, His life displayed the Father perfectly.

Everything He did was what the Father showed Him. What the man Jesus saw with His physical eyes looked the same as what all those who were with Him saw. But He had finely tuned spiritual senses and the eyes of His heart could see the Father working. The way it seemed to work was that he *just happened upon* the people that the Father had assigned to Him for ministry. He walked in sync with the Spirit and those assignments God had for Him presented themselves.

For example, as He was on His way to Jerusalem, "Jesus traveled along the border between Samaria and Galilee. As he was going into a village, ten men who had leprosy met him" (Luke 17:11–12), and He healed them.

Another time, headed from Judea toward Galilee,

> *He had to go through Samaria. So he came to a town in Samaria called Sychar, near the plot of ground Jacob had given to his son Joseph. Jacob's well was there, and Jesus, tired as he was from the journey, sat down by the well. It was about noon. When a Samaritan woman came to draw water, Jesus said to her, "Will you give me a drink?"*
>
> —JOHN 4:4–7

He found Himself in a very specific spot at a certain time when it just happened that a certain woman came to draw water, and He revealed the Father to her.

Later, Jesus was passing through Cana in Galilee on His travels, and this is what happened:

> *There was a certain royal official whose son lay sick at*
> *Capernaum. When this man heard that Jesus had arrived*
> *in Galilee from Judea, he went to him and begged him to*
> *come and heal his son, who was close to death.*
>
> —JOHN 4:46–47

Do you see the pattern? You can see it in every encounter Jesus had with those who needed His ministry. He was just doing life, and ministry found Him. He kept His heart synced to the Father's, and everything the Father had designated Him to do crossed His path. That's how the Father showed the Son what to do.

LIVING SYNCED: RIGHT PLACE, RIGHT TIME

My friend Debra Weitala tells this story:

> In my late twenties, I left my office for the airport. I had a
> couple hours at the darkened gate before my plane left, so
> I settled in to read when a woman unloaded her arms into
> the seat next to me and asked if I would watch her stuff
> while she made a call (pre-cell phone). There was no one
> else at the gate and I nodded.
>
> As she returned she was frustrated that she was at
> the airport so early, commenting that she could have

spent more time with her cousin. Perplexed, she turned to me and said, "Do you have a personal relationship with Christ?" It dawned on her that she wasn't there by accident, and since I was literally the only one at the gate, there must be a purpose for her arrival on the scene.

Having grown up in the church, I said, "Yes." However, when she asked what church I attended, I informed her I didn't believe in organized religion. She responded in love. She began to tell me about her cousin June Hunt (author, counselor, broadcaster) and her cousin's church. I became intrigued not by the church, but by more secular reasons. I thought this might be a networking piece to a better job. Swann Bates gave me her card and suggested I meet her cousin.

When I returned from vacation, I decided to meet June Hunt. I called a friend who had invited me to this church and asked her to take me. She must have been shocked, since she had made the invitation years prior. But once I entered the church I felt the presence of the Holy Spirit, and I couldn't proceed with my intended mission. So I began attending First Baptist Church of Dallas.

One of the pastors at First Baptist of Dallas suggested I take a Bible study class. When he told me the teacher was June Hunt, I thought of her cousin's card in my purse. Apparently I wasn't ready to meet her until I was hungering to know Christ.

So I went to June's house, and as the 50-plus people arrived she introduced herself and asked me when I became a Christian. I told what church I attended growing up and assumed that answered her question. The next week she asked the same question, and again I told her the same thing. Then the following evening, I had to drop something off at her home. In the absence of the rest of the class, June asked me the same question, and I danced around it for the last time. She confronted me with a question: did I know that Jesus wants a personal relationship with me?

When she asked if I wanted Christ to live inside of me, I knew this was the missing piece in my life that I had been trying to fill with work, with escape, with other relationships. She wanted to pray with me, and, to be honest, I didn't hear a word she said because I needed to talk to God myself.

I returned to my apartment and went to my knees and ultimately on my face. I asked God, "Now that I know that your intention has always been to live inside of me, if I have done so much in my flesh that you cannot, I don't want to go on," and at this point He lifted me off the floor, a new creation in Christ.

We, too, can live synced. Just as Jesus called on the power from heaven for the tasks of earth, we have access through Him to that same power. Just as Jesus lived synced to the Father's heart and purposes, we can walk and live in the flow of His Spirit, and those things we have been assigned to accomplish will find us where we are.

POWER WALKING

As we walk out our lives, walk out our faith, walk out our purpose, we can do so in the power supplied from heaven, where your Father rules. "Therefore as you have received Christ Jesus the Lord, *so* walk in Him" (Colossians 2:6 NASB).

Jesus depended on power from on high and refused the lure to act in His own abilities. He refused to turn stone to bread when He was famished after 40 days of fasting, though He had the ability to do so. He waited until the Father sent angels to feed Him. He refused to walk away from the Cross, though He had every right to. He depended on the Spirit to carry Him through to complete obedience. Hebrews 9:14 tells us that He "through the eternal Spirit offered himself unblemished to God." He carried out all His assignments as the conduit through whom the Father worked, not in His own power, though He had the power. He declared,

> *Do not believe me unless I do the works of my Father. But if I do them, even though you do not believe me, believe the works, that you may know and understand that the Father is in me, and I in the Father.*
>
> —JOHN 10:37–38

Because your Father—the same Father who supplied and guided Jesus and showed Him everything He was doing—is in the heavens, He can make heaven's power available to you. When you and I refuse to act in our own flesh and choose instead to depend on the supply from our Father, heaven invades earth.

The design of our flesh—our human capacity and capability—does not allow for the kind of power flow that is available from heaven. The circuitry is too limited to carry the load. Only through the living, present, indwelling Jesus and the wiring of His Spirit can eternal power flow. It matters that our Father is in heaven because it is from heaven that the power and provision come. It matters that we have Jesus in us because the power flows from the Father in heaven, through the Son in us, and is directed by the Spirit to the very moment in the very location where it is required. When we are connected to the right Source, then we just live in the flow.

LIVING SYNCED: BUCKLE YOUR SEAT BELT

I was to be speaking in Dallas at an event that had been on my calendar for a long time, and my plan had always been to drive. At the last minute, a meeting was scheduled in Nashville that would make it impossible for me to drive and arrive on schedule, so I had to book an airline ticket on a very early Friday morning flight. As I booked the ticket on the only flight that would work in my schedule, there were only two seats left, way in the back—not my favorite. I did some grumbling as I reserved that seat.

As I sat in my seat the next morning, the window seat remained empty well into the boarding process, and I got my hopes up. But at the last minute, a young woman made her way down the aisle and claimed the seat. A little more inner grumbling on my part ensued.

As the flight took off and things settled down, the young woman began to cry. She was trying to hold back, but her sobbing became quite obvious. I leaned in to offer any help, and as the story unfolded, it went like this: Her very best friend, who was a pastor's wife in the Dallas area, had passed away after a lengthy illness. She got the word late the night before and booked the only flight available and the only seat left. She was going to her friend's funeral services and to comfort and encourage the young widower. "What can I say to him?" She meant it as a rhetorical question, I think. "He still has a church to lead and minister to."

As it turned out, I had not been widowed for long myself. I was still in the throes of grief, and didn't have much advice to give. But I had one thing. One of the most impactful moments for me during my grief came about six weeks after I lost my husband. I couldn't finish sentences without being in tears. I couldn't sing worship songs without coming unglued. I could barely function. This was my first ministry event since his passing, and I didn't know how I would manage. But I had such an incredible experience that it remains a marker for me on my journey. Though I was an emotional wreck, as I stood on the stage, a Presence came over me so powerful that I could feel the change. I gave my message and was in control of my emotions and able to think clearly and stay in the moment. When I walked down from the stage, I was the same mess I had been before. I had that to tell her. Somehow, when we are doing what we are assigned to do, heaven invades earth and our Father in heaven carries us.

I started the trip feeling inconvenienced and a little grumpy. But I found myself in the right place at the right time and realized that my Father in heaven had engineered the whole thing. As I just lived my life, I found myself in the flow of His plan and His assignment found me.

CHAPTER 6

THE HALLOWED NAME

The first petition in Jesus' Model Prayer is that God's name would be hallowed. The name of God is more than the word or the sound we make with our mouths when we say it. In Hebrew thought, the name of someone stood for his character and person. Theologian Louis Berkhof, in *Systematic Theology*, explains that a name

> stands for the whole manifestation of God in His relation to His people, or simply for the person, so that it becomes synonymous with God. This usage is due to the fact that in oriental thought a name was never regarded as a mere vocable, but as an expression of the nature of the thing designated. . . . In the most general sense of the word, then, the name of God is His self-revelation.

To hallow the name of God, then, is more than simply to say it reverently and not to use it in base ways. It has to do with more than saying the name. It primarily has to do with *living* the name. This petition is an urgent plea that God would hallow His own name, that

He would cause His name to be set apart and treated reverently by the way He reveals Himself through His people. We—His people—are His self-revelation. He tells His story through our stories. It has always been this way. The stories in Scripture are not stories about people, but rather stories about God as He reveals Himself in the lives of people. God is always the main character, and every story's purpose is to reveal God's nature and His action in the lives of His people.

LIVE THE NAME

> *I had concern for my holy name, which the people of Israel profaned among the nations where they had gone. Therefore say to the Israelites, "This is what the Sovereign LORD says: It is not for your sake, people of Israel, that I am going to do these things, but for the sake of my holy name, which you have profaned among the nations where you have gone. I will show the holiness of my great name, which has been profaned among the nations, the name you have profaned among them. Then the nations will know that I am the LORD, declares the Sovereign LORD, when I am proved holy through you before their eyes."*
>
> —EZEKIEL 36:21–23

What profaned the name of the Lord among the nations? Not what the Israelites said about Him or how they used His name in conversation, but rather *how they lived.* He will hallow His name by being proved holy "through you before their eyes."

Keep my commands and follow them. I am the LORD. Do
not profane my holy name, for I must be acknowledged as
holy by the Israelites. I am the LORD, who made you holy
and who brought you out of Egypt to be your God. I am
the LORD.

—LEVITICUS 22:31–33

Again, what profanes the holy name? God's name is profaned by His people not keeping His ways. If the people He set apart ("made you holy") and through whom He displayed His power ("who brought you out of Egypt to be your God") did not live out His commands, His name would be profaned—the opposite of hallowed. His self-revelation is through His people.

We reverence and hallow His name through our lives and our trusting obedience. Sometimes the best way to understand a concept is to look at its opposite. What is the opposite of reverence or hallow? The flipside of reverence is contempt. How has God defined contempt? In Numbers 14, we read the story of the Israelites' refusal to follow God into the Promised Land. They chose to fear the inhabitants of the land rather than to revere God. They had unshakeable faith in the inhabitants' ability to defeat them and no faith in God's ability to deliver them the victory. God called this misplaced faith "contempt." He said to Moses, "How long will these people treat me with contempt? How long will they refuse to believe in me?" (Numbers 14:11). When we refuse to trust God and follow His direction and instead ascribe power to earthly circumstances, we are treating God with contempt. When we focus our faith on God and recognize that earthly circumstances are only the stage for the display of His power, we are revering Him and hallowing His name. It is through our faith-fueled obedience that He hallows His name—reveals and displays Himself.

GOD'S PROOF

God's purpose for His people is that we will be His evidence, His proof. His plan is that we live lives that can only be explained by His living presence in us and through us. He wants our lives to be platforms for His power. When we are so synced to His heart that what comes through us comes from Him, we are His self-revelation. We offer Him our lives through which to hallow His name. Through the prophet Isaiah, God described His people as "everyone who is called by my name, whom I created for my glory, whom I formed and made" (Isaiah 43:7).

Jesus instructed us to "let your light shine before others, that they may see your good deeds and glorify your Father in heaven" (Matthew 5:16). Our good works will glorify the Father. We will do the kinds of works that can only be explained by heaven's power revealed in earth's circumstances.

In the Jewish faith there is a precept called *kiddush ha-Shem*, roughly translated "sanctification of the Name." Any action by a Jew that brings honor, respect, and glory to God is considered to be sanctification of His name, whereas any behavior or action that disgraces, harms or shames God's name is regarded as a *ḥillul ha-Shem* (defamation of the Name).

The prayer for God to hallow His name is really a yielding of our lives to Him for His purposes. It is a surrender of all that we are to all that He is. It is a deliberate abdication of the rule of your own life to His rule. It is a heart's cry that says, "All of You in all of me!"

JESUS: THE FATHER'S SELF-REVELATION

I have brought you glory on earth by finishing the work
you gave me to do.

—JOHN 17:4

Bringing glory, or glorifying, and hallowing are much the same. To glorify God means to put Him on display, to let Him shine out. Jesus brought the Father glory—hallowed His name—by finishing the work the Father assigned Him to do.

"Father, glorify your name!" (12:28). The time for His crucifixion drew near. Jesus, in His humanity, struggled with the ordeal He was facing. He said to His disciples, "Now my soul is troubled, and what shall I say? 'Father, save me from this hour'? No, it was for this very reason I came to this hour. Father, glorify your name!" (vv. 27–28).

His human nature longed for an easier way. But His struggle was put to rest as He subjugated His emotions to the purpose of the Father.

When Jesus first responded to His disciples' request, "Lord, teach us to pray," His circumstances were not as intense. The Cross was not yet looming. In that quieter, less volatile moment, He taught them, "Pray like this: Father, hallow Your name" (author's paraphrase). When His circumstances pressed in on Him, bringing out what was really inside, His heart's cry was still, "Father, glorify Your name!" When He, the Prayer Teacher, teaches you and me to pray, "Father, hallow Your name," it is not just a meaningless or rote recitation. He did not just teach it. He lived it. As you live connected to His heart, you will find that He is fashioning a heart that desires the Father's glory. Underneath all your swirling emotions and the pull of your human nature is the Spirit of the Son, sent into your heart, crying, "Abba, Father! Glorify Your name!" Your will can win out over your emotions. You will find a settled peace as you surrender to your true heart's cry: "Father, glorify Your name. Whatever path it sets me on; whatever 'flesh' must go to the Cross; Father, glorify Your name!"

Jesus offered His every-minute-of-the-day life as the setting in which the Father could hallow His name. Jesus said His disciples,

> *Don't you believe that I am in the Father, and that the Father is in me? The words I say to you I do not speak on my own authority. Rather, it is the Father, living in me, who is doing his work. Believe me when I say that I am in the Father and the Father is in me; or at least believe on the evidence of the works themselves.*
>
> —JOHN 14:10–11

He made the case time and again that the works the Father accomplished through Him were evidence of the Father. Jesus was not bringing the spotlight to bear on Himself, but instead was revealing the Father. Jesus, synced to the Father, was the vehicle through whom the Father worked in the world. Through Jesus, the Father hallowed His name.

Another time, He made a similar claim to the Pharisees who were accusing Him of blasphemy for claiming God as His Father.

> *Do not believe me unless I do the works of my Father. But if I do them, even though you do not believe me, believe the works, that you may know and understand that the Father is in me, and I in the Father.*
>
> —JOHN 10:37–38

Again, His life was proof of the Father's power. Through Jesus, the Father was hallowing His name.

That's how it looks to live synced. Available to Jesus like Jesus was available to the Father. The whole tone of your life will be Him. He will act through you in ways that can't be accomplished by your best efforts or your own abilities. Jesus explained,

> *Very truly I tell you, the* Son can do nothing by himself; *he can do only what he sees his Father doing, because whatever the Father does the Son also does. For the Father loves the Son and* shows him all he does.
>
> —JOHN 5:19–20 (author's emphasis)

He says to His disciples: *"Apart from me you can do nothing"* (15:5, author's emphasis); "Whoever has my commands and keeps them is the one who loves me. The one who loves me will be loved by my Father, and I too will love them and *show myself to them"* (14:21, author's emphasis).

We can live connected to His heart the same way that He lives connected to the Father's heart. The Father's heart in Jesus—Jesus' heart in us—all one.

> *That all of them may be one, Father, just as you are in me and I am in you. May they also be in us so that the world may believe that you have sent me. I have given them the glory that you gave me, that they may be one as we are one—I in them and you in me—so that they be brought to complete unity. Then the world know that you sent me and have loved them even as you have loved me.*
>
> *—JOHN 17:21–23*

When the Father flows through the Son and the Son flows through His people, the world will know that Jesus is the One and Only. The Name will be hallowed. He will be revealed. Jesus said, "I have given them (My people) the glory that you (Father) gave me (Son)." What is the glory that the Father gave the Son, and that the Son now gives to His followers? He explains "that they may be one as we are one: I in them and you in me." That's the glory. Jesus revealed the Father—glorified Him, let Him shine out and become visible—now He has passed that glory on to us. We are to glorify Him, reveal Him, let Him shine out of us. How? By being so synced to Him that it mirrors the way He is synced to the Father.

APPOINTED AND ANOINTED

When God gave instructions for the building of the tabernacle in the wilderness, He was specific and detailed. The structure and all its components were ornate and elaborate. It would take great skill to follow His instructions about how to build what would be His dwelling place among His people—the place where He would put His name (presence). Referring to the Temple, of which the tabernacle was a precursor, the psalmist says, "LORD, I love the house where you live, the place where your glory dwells" (Psalm 26:8) and refers to it as "the dwelling place of your Name" (74:7). His name and His glory are synonymous. His glory—outshining, ebullience, radiance—reveals who He is, as His name is His self-revelation.

So, the Lord gave careful instructions for building His dwelling place, the place where His name would be revealed through every weaving, every stitch, every material, every molding. He also appointed the artisans that would accomplish this monumental task. He called them out by name.

> Then the LORD said to Moses, "See, I have chosen Bezalel son of Uri, the son of Hur, of the tribe of Judah, and I have filled him with the Spirit of God, *with wisdom, with understanding, with knowledge and with all kinds of skills*—to make artistic designs for work in gold, silver and bronze, to cut and set stones, to work in wood, and to engage in all kinds of crafts. Moreover, I have appointed Oholiab son of Ahisamak, of the tribe of Dan, to help him."
>
> —EXODUS 31:1–6 (author's emphasis)

He chose, called, and appointed specific individuals for the task. These were seasoned craftsmen who learned and honed their craft during captivity in Egypt. When it seemed that they were serving taskmasters, they were really under God's tutelage and training. They had been training for generations, as one generation of skilled artisans passed along their skill to the next. He knew their names and called them out to serve Him in a way for which He had equipped them.

But He added to their skill, training, natural ability, and experience. He filled them with the Spirit of God specifically for this task. And He gave special ability beyond natural ability and skill to every worker for each one's particular assignment.

> Also I have given ability *to all the skilled workers to make everything I have commanded you: the tent of meeting, the ark of the covenant law with the atonement cover on it, and all the other furnishings of the tent—the table and its articles, the pure gold lampstand and all its accessories, the altar of incense, the altar of burnt offering and all its utensils, the basin with its stand—and also the woven garments, both the sacred garments for Aaron the priest and the garments for his sons when they serve as priests, and the anointing oil and fragrant incense for the Holy Place. They are to make them just as I commanded you.*
>
> —EXODUS 31:6–11 (author's emphasis)

He has called each of us to be kingdom builders and to hallow His name where we live and work. We each have specific tasks that He assigned and marked out for us before we were born. "For we are

God's handiwork, created in Christ Jesus to do good works, which God prepared in advance for us to do" (Ephesians 2:10).

For those tasks, He called you out by name. Not just, "Hey, somebody!" but instead, called you by your name. That calling typically comes when you simply find yourself where you are supposed to be when you are supposed to be there. You probably don't hear that call in any audible way, but you just find yourself in the middle of it. When you live synced to Jesus, your assignments find you, and you find that you have the particular anointing for that moment. You are prepared and gifted, but you are also anointed. By the time you find yourself in the midst of an appointment, that work has been "prepared in advance for [you] to do." It is ready, ripe. The ground has been tilled for the seed to be planted.

When Jesus' assignments found Him, they were prepared and set up in advance. They didn't come too early in His ministry, or too late. Notice how Jesus seemed to be able to speak great wisdom and depth off-the-cuff, on the spur of the moment. Don't you think that is because He had given great thought in prayer to these things in advance? Not only are His assignments prepared for Him, but also He is prepared for His assignments.

It is the same with us. Synced to Jesus, He will never call us into a moment for which He has not prepared us and prepared for us. Our response to His call in that moment will flow naturally. We won't have to sweat and struggle and anguish. All the pieces come together and dovetail in an instant, and we allow Him to hallow His name through us. These assignments are only occasionally big and dramatic. Usually, it is just the everyday interactions and events as we live our lives in fairly routine ways. We are always on call.

LIVING SYNCED: BE READY

Author Nancy Wilson tells the following story:

> The day arrived for my book signing! What an incredible, faith-filled journey it had been.
>
> Beginning with a desperate prayer, "Lord Jesus, please find a way that I can share the gospel in this country of Turkey."
>
> I had been told that it was illegal to share the gospel with anyone under 18, yet my heart longed for these precious high school students to hear about Jesus. But what about the local believers I could put at risk?
>
> That is when my earnest prayers began. Every morning, prayer walking the city declaring Isaiah 60:1–2, that the light and glory of God would rise in Turkey!
>
> Later in the week, a chance meeting with a radio host landed me an invitation to be his radio guest. With gusto and faith I shared my personal testimony, which included the glorious *gospel!*
>
> People called in and asked about me and the books I'd written in English. Are they in Turkish?
>
> My radio host spoke on my behalf in Turkish, saying, yes, they will be translated and published in Turkish. Later, he informed me of his answer, assuring me that it must be done.
>
> Wow! *Look at the new doors my prayers have opened,* I thought! But, oh my, how can this all happen?

That is where my faith journey continued, one miracle after another—finances, translation, publishing—until this day arrived for my first Turkish book signing. How excited and expectant I was! God had opened this door and I was told the Turkish Book Fair was a big event in Istanbul.

I woke up early that morning and went out for a jog. Coming back, I decided to stop and enjoy the hotel's breakfast buffet. Placing my jacket on a chair, I went to choose from the scrumptious food. Returning to my table, I was surprised when a very dignified and well-dressed man was seated across from my place at the table.

Feeling a bit embarrassed about wearing my jogging attire, I decided to simply enjoy a new acquaintance. As I introduced myself and asked his name. Asking where he was from and why he was here caused me to quickly lose interest in the food. "I am the Ambassador from Iraq to Turkey!"

"Oh my," I said, "that is wonderful! I pray every day for Iraq and the soldiers."

"Why do you care so much?" he asked.

I swallowed hard, and said with sincerity, "I believe the Prince of Peace cares deeply about the people in Iraq, and I have come to know Jesus, the Prince of Peace through a personal relationship." His curiosity was peaked. "Tell me more about this."

In the next half hour, I had the privilege and honor to share my personal testimony of how I was searching for truth, and after studying various world religions, I came to discover who Jesus was . . . the Savior of the world.

As he intently listened, I explained the gospel clearly, and how he, too, could open his heart to receive Jesus as his Savior, when the time came that he believed.

He thanked me profusely, expressing deep gratitude that he had never heard anything like this before! Then he asked me, "What do you do and why are you here?" To his surprise, I said, "I am here for the book fair for my new book in Turkish, and I, too, am an ambassador . . . not for any king, but for the King of kings!"

He smiled as if he understood, we shook hands and we said good-bye. I told him I would continue to pray for his nation and for him to come to know "the Prince of Peace."

After my divine encounter, I did go to the book fair with joy! I had the delight and honor of signing 200 books personally to young "covered" Muslim girls, and giving many others away.

Prayer is the adventure for an "ambassador on assignment."

CHAPTER 7

SEEK THE KINGDOM

"Your kingdom come, your will be done, on earth as it is in heaven." These three lines are all one petition. "Your kingdom come" and "your will be done" and "on earth as it is in heaven" are three ways of saying the same thing. This is a common Hebrew literary device. Each phrase adds to the fullness of understanding, but they are saying the same thing in different ways. It informs us that the kingdom of God is present where the will of God is done. Where the will of God is done, heaven has invaded earth and the kingdom is present.

The kingdom is not something only for the future but is present right now. When we examine the heavenly realms and see the Scripture says the heavenly realms are available as our present-tense reality, we begin to see the kingdom. The kingdom of God—or kingdom of heaven—is the spiritual dimension of our day-to-day experience, and it is where the power is.

Our entering into the kingdom means our being brought into a life in which God rules over all, His will is truly and joyfully done, and all the blessedness that reigns in heaven finds its counterpart here below. As it is written, *"The kingdom of God is . . . righteousness, and peace, and joy in the Holy Ghost"* (Romans 14:17). A third mark of a kingdom is power. *"The kingdom of God is not in word but in power"* (1 Corinthians 4:20). Just think of the work those simple fishermen dared to undertake and were able to accomplish. Think of the weapon with which they had to do their work—the despised Gospel of the crucified Nazarene. Think of all that God brought about through them, and see how the coming of the kingdom brought a new power from heaven. By this power, feeble men were made mighty through God, and the slaves of Satan were made God's holy children.

—ANDREW MURRAY, *On the Holy Spirit*

We are invited to enter the kingdom, or to come into full possession of the kingdom. When we enter into the kingdom, the kingdom enters into us. Where the King rules, the kingdom is active.

"But that is exactly what we are, each of us a temple in whom God lives. God himself put it this way: 'I'll live in them, move into them; I'll be their God and they'll be my people'" (2 Corinthians 6:16, *The Message*).

God rules within so He can manifest himself and His kingdom's power through you and for you. The kingdom is not something we have to talk Him into giving us, or persuade Him of our fitness for, but we enter into it at His invitation. "Do not be afraid, little flock, for your Father has been pleased to give you the kingdom" (Luke 12:32).

"But seek first his kingdom and his righteousness, and all these things will be given to you as well" (Matthew 6:33). What does it mean to seek? It means to look for it everywhere. To be on the lookout for it. To expect to see it at every turn. In every interaction, at every decision, with every word, seek the King's rule and so enter the kingdom.

Jesus' message was summed up in this: "From that time on Jesus began to preach, 'Repent, for the kingdom of heaven has come near'" (4:17). Following His baptism and His 40 days in the desert, when His ministry officially began, He was preaching and demonstrating that the long awaited kingdom of God was now in operation. "Jesus went throughout Galilee, teaching in their synagogues, proclaiming the good news of the kingdom" (v. 23). It summed up the entirety of His message. Everything He taught and everything He did was inviting us to live in the kingdom of God.

"Let Your kingdom come" is a another way of saying, "Let Your will be done on earth as it is in heaven. Right this minute, in this situation, let Your will be done. Right now, hallow Your name through me."

THE KINGDOM IS AT HAND

The Hebrew word that Jesus would likely have used for repent means "to turn" or "to change the way of thinking." "Change your mind," says it partially. But it is not just "change your opinion" or "change your beliefs." More accurately, it means to "reorient your thinking" or "refocus your attention." *Repent* is the first word of the message, and it was spoken as a strong command. Repent! Why? Repent *because* the kingdom of heaven is near. The language does not mean the kingdom is coming, is about to come, or is in the process of coming. Rather, it means the kingdom of heaven *has come*. The kingdom of heaven *is here*. The King James Version of the Bible and the New American Standard Bible both translate *near* as "at hand." The phrase "at hand" means right here, within reach. Right here for the taking. Just reach out and grab hold. The message is this: reorient your thinking and refocus your view because the kingdom of heaven is right here for the taking. Why would we need to reorient and refocus because the kingdom has come? The kingdom of God is invisible. It is not made of earth stuff. If we have our attention and our focus on that which is material and physical, we will not see the kingdom. "So we fix our eyes not on what is seen, but on what is unseen, since what is seen is temporary, but what is unseen is eternal" (2 Corinthians 4:18).

We repent by turning from our sin because we have seen it clearly for what it is, and we have reoriented our hearts toward righteousness. We reorient our thinking so that we understand the heavenly realm is where the power and provision for the material realm originates. When we live in the kingdom, we let heaven supply earth.

In each person and situation that Jesus encountered, He brought the provision of heaven into the setting of earth. In the person of Jesus, the power of heaven moved into the lives and struggles of people. The wisdom to know exactly how to respond to a question so that it hit home with the questioner; the insight to know when one person needed to be challenged to think deeper, and another needed to be comforted and encouraged; the creativity to know how to deliver healing—spittle on clay, a touch, a command, a diagnostic question—in each separate setting. The power of heaven was brought to bear on the situations His people encountered and situations changed in response. He lived synced to the Father's heart, and when earth needed a touch from heaven, it flowed through Jesus.

Think of it like this: You are an astronaut in outer space. This is not your native air. This is not the environment that you are designed to function in. You need some kind of contraption that will supply you with air and air pressure and some form of gravity that will allow you to maneuver in this environment that doesn't meet your needs and will, in fact, be death to you. So, you have a space station and a space suit that supplies your life needs so you can live and move and be in outer space. You might be on Mars, but you are being supplied by Earth's resources.

You live in the material realm, but it is not your home. The material realm is not your native air. As long as you live in a material body in this physical environment, you are always being supplied by the resources of heaven. God has made a way for the kingdom to be available to you every minute of every day. The way He made is the indwelling, present Jesus living in you right now. Jesus is still where heaven and earth meet. Jesus is still the channel through which heaven's resources flow into earth's circumstances. And He is at home in you.

LIVING SYNCED: A GIFT THAT KEEPS ON GIVING

Author Nancy McGuirk, in her book *To Live Is Christ*, tells this story:

> My husband and I visited Cuba in the 1980s on a busi-
> ness trip. The tightly controlled government provided

a wonderful female interpreter and guide who showed us around Havana and other parts of the island nation. The conditions in the country were heartbreaking; we witnessed so many sad and hopeless looks on the faces of the people we met. When it was time to leave, many in our group offered our guide small gifts of appreciation for her service to us—a bracelet, scarf, and other gifts. I remembered I had a small New Testament pocket Bible in my purse, so I pulled our guide to the side and asked if she had ever read the Bible. She said she hadn't, but had heard of the Bible and had always wanted to read it. I gave her an English language New Testament but made one request: that she read and translate it into Spanish for others in her family and community. She said she would. Two years later, an individual from my husband's company returned from a follow-up trip to Cuba with a message for me. He had met the same guide, and she wanted him to convey a message to me about how her life had changed as a result of reading the New Testament I left with her and how she had read it to others as well. (I later learned that she had managed to gain her freedom from the oppressive Communist regime after leaving Cuba.) All I could think of was Isaiah 55:11: "So is my word that goes out from my mouth: *It will not return to me empty, but will accomplish what I desire and achieve the purpose for which I sent it*" (author's emphasis).

HEAVEN'S BREAD SUPPLY

At the time of this occurrence, Jesus' fame and popularity were on the rise. The reports of His healing exploits were everywhere. Crowds pursued Him wherever He went. He had finished several days of ministering to large and needy crowds and was planning for some time with His small group of disciples, but a large crowd followed Him. Some had been with Him for as long as three days. They were in a remote area, and the crowds would need to eat. Here was the situation: 5,000 men, not counting women and children, traveling to Jerusalem for Passover. All coming to hear Jesus, all needy in some way, all would soon need food. The disciples took inventory of the available supply. They discovered just a few loaves of bread and a few fish. They compared what was available to what was needed. There was an insurmountable gap. They saw only one solution: "This is a remote place, and it's already getting late. Send the crowds away, so they can go to the villages and buy themselves some food" (Matthew 14:15). Philip assessed the situation and reached this conclusion: "It would take more than half a year's wages to buy enough bread for each one to have a bite!" (John 6:7). The view from earth revealed a bleak situation, one for which there was no answer in sight.

Enter Jesus. The disciples broke the bad news to Him: "Here is a boy with five small barley loaves and two small fish," and then added their assessment: "but how far will they go among so many?" (v. 9). That's how it looked to the disciples. That's how they told the story. But Jesus had His mind oriented toward the kingdom. He wasn't seeking the solution. He was seeking the kingdom.

Jesus then took the loaves, gave thanks, and distributed to
those who were seated as much as they wanted. He did the
same with the fish.

—JOHN 6:11

Notice that when He gave thanks, there were only the few loaves
and fish in His hands. When He gave thanks, there was not enough.
Then He began to distribute and give away. What does common
sense say to do when you don't have enough? Hoard what you have;
hide it; bury it for safe keeping. But as He gave away, not enough
became more than enough.

> *When they had all had enough to eat, he said to his disci-*
> *ples, "Gather the pieces that are left over. Let nothing be*
> *wasted." So they gathered them and filled twelve baskets*
> *with the pieces of the five barley loaves left over by those*
> *who had eaten.*
>
> — JOHN 6:12–13

Do you see the contrast between Philip's assessment—"It would take
more than half a year's wages to buy enough bread for each one to
have a bite!"—and the reality when the kingdom comes: "Jesus . . .
distributed to those who were seated as much as they wanted"?

Through Jesus, kingdom supply moved into earth's need. The
kingdom's inventory was distributed to earth's inhabitants. When
Jesus is present, the kingdom has come. Living synced to Jesus means
having ready access to everything we need when we need it. The
kingdom is at hand.

LIVING SYNCED: YOU'VE GOT MAIL

Author Lynn Eib tells this story of how the kingdom was revealed in the moment she needed it.

> Many years ago, my pastor husband and I made a $1,000 "faith promise" to our church's missions giving. This was to be over and above our tithe, and we had absolutely no way to pay it on our own. But one day I got a letter telling me I had won first prize in an international writing competition, and enclosed was a check for $1,000. Turns out a local fire company had entered my newspaper series from the year before on the "dangers of firefighting." I knew nothing about being entered, and it was the largest award anyone won on the paper that year! God is amazing!

Lisa Miller Reiff tells this story of God's provision showing up when the material realm offered no answers.

> One year ago our family was in dire straights financially as a result of my husband's longtime issues with pain and the inability to work steadily—the result of a car accident. We were behind on our mortgage and heading into summer when my income decreased significantly. Then our car's engine completely died, needing to be replaced, requiring way more money than we had any access to.
>
> The next week one of my newer voice students asked how I was doing, and I briefly mentioned our car had died

(something I wouldn't normally do). Later that night I received an email from her father, who I had never met, saying he heard about our car and had just mailed a check for $10,000 to help with our transportation issues. Then after a phone call and conversation the next day, he met my husband at a car dealership, and 90 minutes later he drove off the lot with a brand new Ford Escape, a gift in addition to the money this man had already given us. Total miracle—when we were at the end of ourselves and no hope but God.

Jenel Moline tells of kingdom riches in earth's circumstances:

I had been working in a ministry for three years without pay. I was finally at the point of looking for a paying job and was starting to feel discouraged. I remember putting my head in my hands, *OK, Lord, what next?* I had the thought to just go check my mail. So I walked out to my mail and there were two green business-size envelops with a return address but no name. I opened the first envelope, and a $100 dollar bill "fell in to my lap." The same thing happened with the second envelope. It felt as if the Lord was saying to me, "Just trust Me in the next step. I will provide."

Seek the kingdom. Watch for it everywhere. Expect to find it. When the material realm presents no solution, seek the kingdom. Jesus is in you, and Jesus is the vehicle through whom kingdom supply is transferred into earth's circumstances. Our Father in heaven, let Your kingdom come right here, right now, in the middle of this mess.

CHAPTER 8

TO WILL HIS WILL

*T*he petition for the kingdom is expounded by "let your will be done." The second phrase adds to the understanding of the first. When God's specific, intervening plan is enacted, the kingdom comes. With these few words, the Prayer Teacher shows us an astounding truth about the role of prayer. Prayer is the conduit that brings the direct, intervening, specific power and provision of God into the circumstances of earth.

This is not an arm's-length, passive prayer. Rather, it is an assertive, proactive prayer. Earlier, you looked at the fact that God's work is finished, but that finished work must come from the spiritual realm (heaven) to the material realm (earth). Prayer is how the finished will of God comes into the circumstances of earth. Prayer releases the power of God to accomplish the purposes of God. Jesus is not teaching us to pray some generic, blanket prayer, but instead He wants us to use this prayer in every specific, minute detail of our lives. We can pray, "In this detail, Father, let Your finished work be expressed. In this situation, on this day, at this time let Your sovereign rule take direct effect. For this need, let everything available in heaven be manifested on the earth." When, through prayer, God's people access the power and the plan of God, they can be confident that God's intervening power will take effect and His specific plan will be worked out.

What peace can be yours when you recognize the tool God has put at your disposal! God's work is finished, and prayer will bring it into your circumstances. Soul-Sabbath means resting in His finished work and trusting His Word that prayer will cause His plan to take effect.

His will in every situation will lead to restoration, healing, and wholeness. You can trust that His plan will reflect His love for you. You can find soul rest in knowing that His desire for you and for those you love is to prosper you and not to harm you, to give you a hope and a future (Jeremiah 29:11). "Truly my soul finds rest in God; my salvation comes from him"(Psalm 62:1). Rest in the fact that He is the source of a perpetual, never ending deliverance. In everything that comes into your life, He is actively and aggressively acting on your behalf. You are safe. In Him, you can find rest for your soul.

WILLING

Do not conform to the pattern of this world, but be trans-formed by the renewing of your mind. Then you will be able to test and approve what God's will is—his good, pleasing and perfect will.

—ROMANS 12:2

When you discover the great truth that prayer activates the specific will of God in a situation, the thought will be restful only if you have moved to the place of willing the will of God. Often we can have an underlying sense that God's will is something we have to bear up under or settle for.

God's will, we think, is difficult and oppressive. In Romans 12:2, Paul described God's will with three words: good, pleasing, and perfect. Greek words used might be translated "beneficial," "bringing pleasure," and "a perfect fit." Only when you come to know God through experience—when you have put His will to the test and have firsthand understanding that it is good—can you find rest and peace in the thought of His will being done. But the secret to experiencing God this way is that you first have to obey Him and surrender to Him in order to put His will to the test. You have to take the one step in front of you. You have to abandon the old familiar flesh-ways.

You have to set your face like flint in the direction He is pointing you, making no provision to turn back. Only then can you say, "Your promises have been thoroughly tested, and your servant loves them" (Psalm 119:140).

In Scripture, words involving the senses describe how you will know God. For example, "Taste and see that the Lord is good" (Psalm 34:8); "I pray that the eyes of your heart may be enlightened" (Ephesians 1:18); and, "Whoever has ears to hear, let them hear" (Mark 4:9).

Why do you think God used sense words? I think it is because those things that you know by your senses, you know because of firsthand experience. Could you, for example, describe the taste of a fresh strawberry to someone who has never tasted a fresh strawberry? Could you describe the sound of rain or the smell of the ocean to a person who has never heard rain or smelled the ocean?

What you know by means of your senses, you know because you have experienced it. So it is with the deep things of God. You must first know Him by experience. Then you will know with certainty that His will is good, pleasing, and perfect. God reveals His will progressively. He unfolds it obedience by obedience. "The path of the righteous is like the morning sun, shining ever brighter till the full light of day" (Proverbs 4:18). Each obedience sets the stage for the next step. As you keep putting His promises to the test, you will discover that where there used to be hesitancy and uncertainty, there is now a settled confidence. Your steps that started out halting and tentative are now sure and steady. Little by little, step-by-step, you prove the will of God to be good, pleasing, and perfect.

Once you know for yourself that God's will is desirable, you will be able to trust that His will for all situations is equally desirable. You will learn to pray with expectant joy, let "your kingdom come, your will be done, on earth as it is in heaven" (Matthew 6:10). You will rest in His will completely.

You can live at rest when the attitude of your heart becomes, "He is the LORD; let him do what is good in his eyes" (1 Samuel 3:18). This thought is echoed by Jesus. "Yes, Father, for this way was well-pleasing in Your sight" (Matthew 11:26 NASB).

"For I have come down from heaven not to do my will but to do the will of him who sent me" (John 6:38). Jesus, while on earth in His physical form, showed us what a life completely abandoned to God's will looked like. His fully surrendered life was a life through which all the power of God freely flowed. His very words tell us that time after time He *chose* the will of God over His human will.

He yielded His will to God's every moment. "For I have come down from heaven not to do my will but to do the will of him who sent me." Because He chose the Father's will, He worked the Father's works. "It is the Father, living in me, who is doing his work. Believe me when I say that I am in the Father and the Father is in me; or at least believe on the evidence of the works themselves" (14:10–11).

The Father's miracles flowed onto the earth and into the lives of individuals through Jesus. Jesus' surrender to God's will made it possible for the Father's finished work to be manifested on earth. Jesus is far more to us than an example. The very life He lived on earth through His human nature He now lives in me and in you. Just as His life on earth was marked by an absolute surrender to the Father's will, so His life in me forms the same desire in me—not my will, but His will. God is actively and energetically working in you to create desires that match His will. "It is God who works in you to will . . . his good purpose" (Philippians 2:13). Your will is progressively being fused into oneness with His.

He is producing in me and in you the complete surrender to the will of the Father that is the hallmark of His life. As He works mightily in us, our heart's desire becomes, "Not my will. Your will. All I want is what You want. Let Your will be done."

A PERFECT FIT

God's will fits you. You were created and designed for His will. He didn't create you then try to find a way to use you. He created you for a purpose. That purpose is one that will fulfill, motivate, and drive you. Outside the will of God for you is dissatisfaction and emptiness.

Recording artist and author Babbie Mason, in her book *Embraced by God*, shares her own journey to God's purpose and will for her life. To say that Babbie has a great musical gift is an understatement. She is wildly talented and gifted. As a young woman, her dream was to be signed by a secular record label. In pursuit of that ambition, she wandered from her roots. She grew up in her father's church, singing, leading the choir, and teaching Sunday School. But her talents offered her the opportunity to sing in bars. It had no real appeal to her, but she thought it was the road to realizing her dream. Her divided life—trying to fit in with her unbelieving friends and still be the person she had always been—created dissonance in her life. She "played a good game, but in her heart she knew the truth. She was a hypocrite. And the lifestyle she thought would help her fit in actually made her feel isolated and alone."

Obviously, Babbie turned her life around. She was awarded a music scholarship to a Christian university and became a lead singer in that university's Christian singing group, which led to the recording of her first album. And everything flowed from there. When she lined up with God's plan for her, she found the life that fit. And she wears it beautifully.

God's will is what you were born for. It fits you. Let me illustrate with the parable of the high-heeled, pointy-toed shoes.

Once upon a time, I found a pair of beautiful high-heeled, pointy-toed shoes. I immediately knew that I could not live a happy or fulfilled life without them. So, I bought them. I decided to debut them when the most people would have the opportunity to admire them, so I wore them on a day when I had meetings all day long.

I got just the response I was hoping for. "Those are beautiful shoes!" But by midday, I did not love the shoes as much, and by the end of the day I just wanted to get them off my feet. When I got home that evening, I peeled the shoes off my feet. I compared the shape of the shoe to the shape of my foot and had an epiphany. My foot was not destined for that shoe.

When we try to live outside God's will for us, we are trying to squeeze into a mold of someone else's design. God's plan for you will not squeeze you from the outside, but will shape you from the inside. It will fit. It will be the way that is best for you.

> *Who, then, are those who fear the LORD? He will instruct them in the ways they should choose. They will spend their days in prosperity, and their descendants will inherit the land.*
>
> —PSALM 25:12–13

> *This is what the LORD says — your Redeemer, the Holy One of Israel: "I am the LORD your God, who teaches you what is best for you, who directs you in the way you should go."*
>
> —ISAIAH 48:17

HIDE AND SEEK?

God's will is not tricky or hidden. He puts it right out in the open and writes it in neon lights. He has more interest in seeing you living in His will than you do in finding it. When we live synced to the heart of Jesus, God's will finds us where we are.

Sometimes we have a sense of God's will as something we have to figure out. Much of the time when we are trying to "know God's will," what we really want to know is the future. God will not be your fortune-teller. He won't tell you what is going to happen in the future. He tells you what to do right now. He shows you the next step, not several steps down the road. Follow what you know right now.

We have a tendency to extrapolate and project into the future what we think should happen, but the future surprises us. If we are not open to whatever comes next—anticipated or not—then we will be off-kilter when life takes twists and turns we did not expect. And it will. Knowing God's will does not mean knowing the future or what the future holds.

It is not uncommon for a person whose life takes an unexpected turn to think she has missed God's will. That person can look back over her life and revisit decisions she has made along the way and second guess any of them. "If only I had chosen differently here, or there, things would have turned out differently." But God's plan isn't predictable.

Whatever step you need to take right now, you will know it when you need to know it. Sometimes, the "knowing" might feel like a certainty. "I just know." Other times, it may feel like you are closing your eyes and picking. But God is there, directing. He knows how to close doors and open doors. He knows how to introduce new information. He knows how to direct your thoughts and ideas. He knows how to influence you. He understands what will get your attention.

Sometimes people worry that a major decision they made in their lives before they were attentive to the Lord might have put their lives off course. But God is not trapped in linear time. Even back then, He was responding to the heart He knew was in the making. He heard today's prayer way back then. "Before they call I will answer; while they are still speaking I will hear" (Isaiah 65:24).

God is not hiding or disguising His will for you. He knows how to make it known.

A situation that sometimes creates anxiety about knowing God's will is when there seems to be several equally good options and none of them appear to be an obvious choice. People look at that kind of situation a couple of different ways. One approach is that it doesn't matter which choice you make. Any of the choices will be fine and God will adjust His plan to coincide with your choice. Another approach is that only one of the choices will be God's will and if you accidentally make the wrong one, you will be off course for the rest of your life.

Here is what I believe. I believe that one of the choices among the many will be the step that takes you down the path God designed for you, but you don't have to stress about missing it. From your side, you can relax and make the decision as if any one of the good decisions will be fine, and it will turn out that you have made exactly the right decision. God is big like that. "And I will put my Spirit in you and move you to follow my decrees and be careful to keep my laws" (Ezekiel 36:27). When you live synced to the heart of Jesus, His Spirit in you will move you in the direction of His will, "For it is God who is at work in you, both to will and to work for *His* good pleasure" (Philippians 2:13 NASB). The joy of living synced is that you don't have to be on a frantic search for God's will. As you walk out your life, God's will chases you down and finds you where you are.

LIVING SYNCED: YOU NEVER KNOW

Jeff Eckart, founder of Claim Your Campus, tells this story.

> Professor Todd Guy changed my life. In college as a freshman at Indiana Wesleyan University, on a dare to impress a girl, I auditioned for University Chorale. Having never sung in public before, I called the bluff of my friend who set up the audition and showed up to sing, thinking there was no way I would ever make it. Thank God this man saw something in me and said yes to Jeff Eckart, adding me to the bass section mid-year. When I made Chorale, I didn't have a clue what I had gotten myself into. Todd Guy's standard for excellence and example of leadership literally changed the direction of my future and course of my life. I became chaplain after one semester, and the musical opportunities opened up from then on. If not for that "yes," I've often wondered where I'd be in life.

God has a way of getting you to the right place at the right time. It's His business to do that. Your job is to live synced. Living, breathing, walking out this prayer: let Your will be done.

SYNCING EARTH TO HEAVEN

The final phrase of this petition says, "on earth as it is in heaven." Psalm 119:89 says, "Forever, O Lord, Your word is settled in heaven" (NASB). By means of prayer, we are bringing into earth that which is already settled in heaven. This petition that Jesus prays is showing us again what a forceful and dynamic act prayer is: reaching into the heavenly realms and pulling God's power and provision through the gap and into the circumstances of earth. It shows us that Jesus understood prayer to be the key to how earth's circumstances are synced to heaven's power. God wants to do His intervening will in every situation, in every moment, in every circumstance.

CHAPTER 9

DAY BY DAY

Our own personal need.

❧

The next petition that Jesus prayed was, "Give us today our daily bread." Each petition is going to be compatible with the others, so this petition that switches from God's will and kingdom to our needs, including our physical needs, is not out of place. Jesus prayed this. Prayer is intended to access all the provision that God has for us, and that includes our physical needs. But the way He prays this petition gives us much insight into what it means to live synced to Jesus' heart the way He lived synced to the Father's heart.

God created us so that we have needs. He could have designed us to be self-sufficient. He could have made us, for example, like a turtle, carrying our shelter around with us as. But He made us with needs that act as entry points for Him. Our needs are to drive us to His supply.

HEAVEN SUPPLIES EARTH'S NEEDS

Let's look at the passages where Jesus talks about the Father's care for our daily needs and see that He offers the kingdom as the answer.

I feel sure that Jesus was not simply teaching truths He knew as theory but truths He knew as His own reality. He did not spring from the womb with all knowledge. He gained it as He went. He gained knowledge as He studied Scripture and as He experienced the truth it taught. So, when you hear Jesus teach these concepts, keep in mind that He had experience in His life that brought these truths home to Him.

Jesus progressively matured, just as all humans do. He experienced all the developmental stages. "And the child grew and became strong; he was filled with wisdom, and the grace of God was on him" (Luke 2:40). The Greek word translated *grew* indicates a progressive growth. It is the same word used to describe the growth of plants. It is in the imperfect tense, which indicates continuous action begun in the past. The phrase "was filled" is in a Greek tense that indicates a continuous or repeated action. Jesus went through a process of maturing. He grew, stage by stage, becoming progressively stronger. He was continuously being filled with wisdom. He *learned* that the Father would supply every need.

> Then Jesus said to his disciples: "Therefore I tell you, do not worry about your life, what you will eat; or about your body, what you will wear. For life is more than food, and the body more than clothes. Consider the ravens: They do not sow or reap, they have no storeroom or barn; yet God feeds them. And how much more valuable you are than birds! Who of you by worrying can add a single hour to your life? Since you cannot do this very little thing, why do you worry about the rest? Consider how the wild flowers grow. They

do not labor or spin. Yet I tell you, not even Solomon in all
his splendor was dressed like one of these. If that is how God
clothes the grass of the field, which is here today, and tomor-
row is thrown into the fire, how much more will he clothe
you—you of little faith! And do not set your heart on what
you will eat or drink; do not worry about it. For the pagan
world runs after all such things, and your Father knows
that you need them. But seek his kingdom, and these things
will be given to you as well. Do not be afraid, little flock,
for your Father has been pleased to give you the kingdom."

—LUKE 12:22–32

Jesus is assuring us that God, who made us with needs as part of our
makeup, is prepared to meet those needs. Notice how He wraps up
this teaching on the Father's attention to our physical needs. After
opening it with, "Do not worry," He brings it to a close with, "Do not
be afraid, little flock, for your Father has been pleased to give you the
kingdom." He considers this meeting of material needs part of giving
you the kingdom. The invisible kingdom has visible proof in your
life. He wants it that way. Jesus, who lived synced to the Father, knew
by experience that the kingdom would supply His every need as He
walked in obedience to His call.

JUST ASK

Ask and it will be given to you . . . For everyone who asks
receives.

—MATTHEW 7:7–8

God invites to draw upon His resources for daily needs—physical, emotional, and spiritual. God will provide for you in a practical way. He created our earthbound, time-bound frame and is prepared to meet your every need. God does not have a set of resources with fixed limits. His riches cannot be depleted if used too often. He pleads with you to come to Him in every circumstance, and to come again and again. He is never tired of hearing from you and providing for you. He rejoices over you and rejoices in doing good things for you. If something touches you, it touches Him. You are the apple of His eye. He dotes on you and longs to lavish His love and wealth on you. He wants you, by a choice of your free will, to turn to Him and accept all He wants to give. He waits for you to respond to His generosity by asking.

Jesus highlights the simplicity of supplication by saying, "Ask and it will be given to you . . . For everyone who asks receives." The Greek word translated "ask" is used to ask for something to be given, not done. It is the simplest, most straightforward picture of asking for something you need. Jesus elaborates on this principle further in the following verses.

> Which of you, if his son asks for bread, will give him a stone? Or if he asks for a fish, will give him a snake? If you, then, though you are evil, know how to give good gifts to your children, how much more will your Father in heaven give good gifts to those who ask him!
>
> —MATTHEW 7:9–11

The purest, most unselfish love I have is for my children. For them, I would lay down my life without thinking twice. Their needs are more important than my own. Without flinching, I would make any sacrifice for their happiness. A parent's love for his or her children, in the best of cases, most closely resembles God's love for us. To even begin to understand God's love for us, we would have to take the highest love we know and multiply it by infinity. If you would give good gifts to your children, how much more would God give to His? I don't have to be convinced to give my children what they need. I want to meet their needs. God "richly blesses all who call on him" (Romans 10:12).

Your asking should be anxiety free. "Do not worry about your life" (Matthew 6:25). Jesus tells you that God is aware of your material needs. You can simply ask for your daily needs to be met without having to remind God, and then focus your attention on the kingdom of God and His righteousness. God wants to free you from anxiety about your daily needs so that you will be able to focus on Him.

God knows what you need before you ask Him (see Matthew 6:8). Before you call, He has prepared the answer. You may be caught off guard in your need, but God is not. The purpose of your supplication is not to inform God. The purpose of your supplication is to accept that which God wants to offer. One day one of my sons had an embarrassing incident occur at school. I was told about it by a neighbor who happened to see it. As soon as I heard, I knew that he needed to be encouraged and loved and would need me to help him put it into perspective. All day I planned how I could help him when he came home from school and told me about it. I was not only prepared but also eager to help him. To my surprise and disappointment, he did not tell me about it right away. I had determined that I should wait until he brought it up. It was several days before he told me.

During those days I was longing to give him what he needed. I waited eagerly for him to give me access to his need. It was during these few days that God told me, "This is how I feel when you do not turn to Me in every need. I am overflowing with love toward you and long for you to come to Me and accept My provision for every detail of your life. I have everything prepared and am only waiting for you to ask." By asking, you are syncing your life to His supply. You will find that what you need is there when you need it.

LIVING SYNCED: WHAT YOU NEED WHEN YOU NEED IT

Peggy Ware Stahl tells this story about her father, the late Dr. Russell Ware, as he prepared for ministry:

> My dad enrolled in Baylor to be a minister (free tuition in the late 1930s) but had no money and no way to get there for his first semester. His family was so poor they didn't have much furniture or even a study lamp. A family he didn't know called and said they were taking their son there and asked if he needed a ride from Beaumont to Waco. Once there, he worked to pay for books and his rooming house but had little money for food. One day, while he was waiting for a bus, a woman came out of her house across the street and invited him to come eat with her—"cooked too much," she said. After that she'd often invite him in to eat when she saw him at the bus stop. He would buy a hot dog for a meal when he could scrounge

up a quarter, so having a full meal was a treat. When the first "blue norther" hit that fall, he ran out of the rooming house and planned to run all the way to school because he had no coat and would freeze standing at the bus stop. On the steps of the house, he met the postman, who had a large box to deliver to him. In it was the first overcoat he would ever own, sent by his aunts in Houston. He didn't own a Bible during the time he went to Baylor and was presented one at his ordination service by the ordination committee. He always said he was amazed that he got through Baylor with so little money, but he always got what he needed when he really needed it.

Sandra Clark Barnes tells this story from her days as a college student. A women's group from her home church, First Baptist Church of Tulsa, Oklahoma—Woman's Missionary Union (WMU)—were helping support her through seminary and sent occasional care packages.

> While in seminary, I had a list of things I needed at the store, but no money to buy them with. I picked up my mail that day and everything on the list, plus expensive perfume and a hair dryer was in a gift box from the WMU of First Baptist Church of Tulsa!

Author Pam Farrel tells this story about how God provided a car when she and her husband needed it:

We were in college, newlyweds with no money. Our car died. We rode bikes everywhere for months. Each week our youth group kids would pray for God to provide a car. By faith they bought us a bumper sticker for the yet-to-be car. It read, "I believe in miracles." After six months, one day we got a call. One of the great grandmothers of one of our teens went to be with Jesus, and no one in the family needed her car. It needed a brake job. If we could come up with $37, it was ours. That is all we had in the bank! That old Impala carried us all the way through the rest of college and seminary.

DAY BY DAY

God is very focused on keeping us present in the moment instead of worrying into the future. That's where fear gets a foothold. When we try to live tomorrow today, what God wants to do today gets lost in the haze of an unknowable tomorrow. When my husband was suffering with terminal cancer, I learned this lesson at a new depth. Live today, and don't let tomorrow's possibilities rob you of today's joys. I wrote in my blog:

Right now, he is pretty mobile and much more independent than he has been for several weeks. We are in a good time . . . probably a reprieve before the next effects begin. We are enjoying this day and not worrying about what the next day will bring. This kind of living is what Jesus had in mind when He said, "Therefore do not worry about tomorrow, for tomorrow will worry about itself. Each day has enough trouble of its own" (Matthew 6:34). How silly to add tomorrow's issues to today's activity. How wasteful to miss the pleasure of today because tomorrow might have new challenges in it. We have learned that when the trouble arrives, the grace to deal with it comes along with it. When you worry about it and anticipate it, the grace to handle it is missing. But when it comes, then comes strength. Grace meets you where you stand.

"This is the day the LORD has made; let us rejoice and be glad in it" (Psalm 118:24 ESV). This day. This very day. God has made it—He has scheduled it and arranged it and fit it together hour by hour and minute by minute. I will rejoice in *this* day and in every detail God has placed into it.

Today is all we've got. Be present to today. Receive with joy the supply for today.

joy

Child, I have provided enough for this day. Don't reach into tomorrow and try to live tomorrow on today's strength. Embrace this day and its provision. You don't have what you need for tomorrow? It's not tomorrow yet.

— JENNIFER KENNEDY DEAN,

Conversations With the Most High

See a similar dynamic in a story from the Old Testament when the Lord fed Elijah through a nearly destitute widow. For three years the Lord had been supernaturally feeding Elijah by sending ravens with food. When the brook from which he had been drinking dried up, the Lord gave Elijah a new command. I wrote about this in my book *The Power of Small*:

> Eventually the brook dried up. God said, "Go at once to Zarephath in the region of Sidon and stay there. I have directed a widow in that place to supply you with food" (1 Kings 17:9). Previously, God had commanded the ravens to feed Elijah, and now He has commanded a certain widow to feed him. God had many ways that he could have fed and nourished Elijah. The ravens could still have fed him. Or, this was the same God who had made water gush from a rock and caused manna to appear every morning. He could still do that. But He wanted to provide for Elijah through a certain widow.
>
> How was Elijah to know which widow? As it turned out, when he arrived at the town gate, a widow was there gathering wood. He asked her for some water, and as she was going to get water, Elijah added a request: "And a little bread?" As the story unfolds, it is unmistakable that this is the very widow God has commanded to supply Elijah with food, but she doesn't know she has been commanded. When Elijah asks for the bread, she reveals her situation. She doesn't have any bread. All she has is a handful of flour and a little oil. Just enough to make her and her son a small meal so they can eat it and then lie down to die. She is at the end of her provision. There is no more and she sees no

possible way to get more. This is the widow God has commanded to feed Elijah. The one who was fresh out of food.

Elijah told her to ignore her lack of provision and act as if she had plenty. He told her to go make a small cake of bread for him from her almost empty supply and then make one for herself and her son. Sounds reasonable. She was almost out of food, so she should share that food with one more person. Stretch it further. As soon as she obeyed the Lord, provision began. The jar of flour was not used up and the jug of oil did not run dry. Every time she needed flour and oil, flour and oil were there.

Why did God command this destitute widow to give out of the little she had to provide for the Lord's prophet? So that she could obtain the blessing that giving brings. So that she could receive in the measure she gave. So that she could set in motion the kingdom law that releases the Lord's abundant and perfect provision in response to obedience.

Again, when it looks in the material realm as if there is no supply, and you can't see any way for supply to come, just sit back and relax. You don't have to find the right lever to push or work your way through a tricky maze to find God's answer. Seek the kingdom and all these things will be added to you as well (Matthew 6:33). In those instances, I pray something like this: "Here I am. Do that thing You do. Position me where Your blessing flows."

THE MANNA PLAN

When Rabbi Jesus spoke to His Jewish listeners and taught them to pray for daily bread, what do you think came to mind? Manna. Manna was central to their understanding of God's special work in their lives. The Jews expected the Messiah to be a second Moses and that He would perform signs that were consistent with the signs that came through Moses. One of the central expectations for the Messiah was that He would give them manna, bread that comes down from heaven. The latter Redeemer (Moses is the former redeemer), the rabbis taught, will make manna descend for them.

Notice how they present this challenge to Jesus, implying that He should prove He is Messiah by reproducing the signature work of Moses:

> So they asked him, "What sign then will you give that we may see it and believe you? What will you do? Our ancestors ate the manna in the wilderness; as it is written: 'He gave them bread from heaven to eat.'"
>
> —JOHN 6:30–31

Manna was first "bread from heaven." In light of how we have explored the concept of heaven, what does that mean? Does it mean bread that rained down from the sky? No, it means bread that was available in the invisible realm, then moved into the material realm at exactly the right moment. Manna did not have its origins on earth. It was fully supplied from heaven. During the manna years, when an Israelite went to bed at night, there would be no sign of manna anywhere. He could look under every rock, around every corner, and as far as he could travel, and there would be no evidence of manna. But when morning came, manna was there for the taking. The substance of heaven had moved into the environment of earth.

The second distinguishing characteristic of manna was that it was enough for today. Any Israelite who tried to secure the next day's supply from that day's manna found that it spoiled and became useless. God is training His people in His ways. You will have what you need when you need it. It is a trust issue. You can live in anxiety or you can live at rest. You can know by faith what you can't see with your eyes. In some area of your life—finances, health, emotional strength—God is providing for you using the manna method. Somewhere in your life, you are learning great and valuable lessons as God teaches you by manna.

Let's look at the strategy. Why does God use the manna method?

He humbled you, causing you to hunger and then feeding you with manna, which neither you nor your ancestors had known, to teach you that man does not live on bread alone but on every word that comes from the mouth of the LORD.

—DEUTERONOMY 8:3

His goal is to teach you how to live synced, how to walk in the flow of His provision without anxiety. Let's understand the method. "He humbled you." Being humbled doesn't mean God desires to wreck and humiliate you, but instead desires to bring you to the end of yourself. Over my life, when I have found myself in situations that I could not fix or manage, for which I had no resources, I was brought to the deeper realization that apart from Jesus, I can do nothing. I get a right view of myself. I know my only hope is to live synced to His heart, letting Him supply my needs out of His riches. "And my God will meet all your needs according to the riches of his glory in Christ Jesus" (Philippians 4:19).

I learn again that Jesus is where heaven and earth meet so that heaven's supply can flow into earth's circumstances. I am reminded that I have a desperate dependence on the living, present Jesus for my every need. Jesus lived synced to the Father's heart and in full awareness that the Father was His everything and His complete supply. He describes Himself as "gentle and humble in heart" (Matthew 11:29). To come to the end of yourself and be entirely dependent on Him is beneficial and freeing. It is hard work to try to do for yourself what only He can do for you. To find rest, embrace humility.

"He humbled you, causing you to hunger and then feeding you with manna, which neither you nor your ancestors had known" (Deuteronomy 8:3). He let "hunger" be part of your experience so that He could "feed" you in a new way, a way you had not known before. If you had never known the need for manna, then you would never know that manna exists. He doesn't give manna for entertainment value or to amaze and amuse you. He gives manna to meet your needs, releasing heaven's substance in earth's environment.

"To teach you that man does not live on bread alone but on every word that comes from the mouth of the Lord" (v. 3). He brings you to the end of yourself, so that He can feed you with manna, to teach you that you live by what God speaks. "Let there be" . . . and there is. In Israel's manna years, every day from the heavens God said, "Let there be manna" and there was manna. God does not strain or struggle to supply your need. He just says, "Let there be." When the angel announced to Mary that she, a virgin, would bear a son, He concluded His message by saying, "No word from God shall be without power *or* impossible of fulfillment (Luke 1:37 AMP). God will not speak a word that He does not have the power to perform. Mary's response was, "I am the Lord's servant . . . May your word to me be fulfilled" (v. 38). Synced to the heart of Jesus, we can always be in that humble state of mind—"I am the Lord's servant"—coupled with the trusting heart—"Let whatever You say about my situation be done." Then allow the Lord to meet your needs as He desires, in His way and at His time.

LIVING SYNCED: JUST IN TIME

Jack and Emily had a tough year. Jack lost his job and was seriously injured in an accident. They were barely scraping by but had managed to keep shelter in place for their family. Now that was coming to an end. They were being evicted, and it was just a few nights before the eviction date that they met with their prayer group. This was Tuesday, and they would be evicted the following Monday morning. Prayer group prayed fervently, but no one had any ideas about what to do. Sunday morning, a member of the prayer group woke up with a strong leading to share the dilemma with his Sunday School class. In the class that morning was a couple who were moving out of their home into the wife's mother's home to care for her and did not want to sell their house. Before Monday morning came, the Lord provided through His people. Years passed and things improved. And in the end, Jack and Emily bought the house.

What you need when you need it. Live synced, and discover the wonder of the manna method.

CHAPTER 10

LET IT GO

The next petition is "Forgive us our debts, as we also have forgiven our debtors" (Matthew 6:12). Jesus is teaching us how He prays, but remember, Jesus never sinned and therefor never needed to confess sin. Yet He includes this in the outline for how He prays. That's how completely He identifies with us. He never sinned in either thought or action, yet He so identified with us that He felt the weight of our sins. He came to take our sins on His shoulders and bear them in His body on the Cross. "'He himself bore our sins' in his body on the cross" (1 Peter 2:24).

> *Surely he took up our pain and bore our suffering, yet we considered him punished by God, stricken by him, and afflicted. But he was pierced for our transgressions, he was crushed for our iniquities; the punishment that brought us peace was on him, and by his wounds we are healed.*
>
> —ISAIAH 53:4–5

He was doing in those hours of prayer what He did at the Cross. "Father, forgive them" (Luke 23:34). Pleading our case. Identifying with our weakness and sin so fully that He felt its burden.

WE CLEAN UP NICELY

Unless we recognize our own sin, we won't walk and live in the peace and joy that forgiveness should bring. Because sin does not fit us, the sins in our lives diminish us and steal our joy and our peace. Sin is harmful to us. God hates our sin because He loves us.

Because the Cross accomplished everything necessary for our sins to be forgiven, all we have to do is turn and embrace the work done on our behalf. We can confess our sins and be forgiven and live with clean hearts. Don't you love the feeling of being clean?

We have to let the Holy Spirit do His convicting work in us, showing us the places where we are missing out on all that God has for us because we are choosing instead to cling to sin. If we are synced to the Spirit, then His slightest whispers and His warnings aren't hard to hear. He can direct us around the land mines the enemy has planted in our path. Living synced means living free. We won't get to the place this side of eternity where we don't ever sin, but we can be free from living bound to sin. We can learn to live with such sensitivity to the Spirit and such craving for the fullness of the presence of Jesus that we quickly correct course. We can be continually growing in our ability to respond to the Spirit's conviction.

Synced to the heart of Jesus, He will impart to us His own hatred of sin and its warping influence, and His overcoming power can flow through us just for the asking. His life flowing through us, syncing us to Him, produces in us a pure heart—the essential element for experiencing the fullness of His power.

> *Create in me a clean heart, O God, and renew a steadfast spirit within me.*
>
> —PSALM 51:10 (NASB)

> *Who may ascend the mountain of the LORD? Who may stand in his holy place? The who has clean hands and a pure heart.*
>
> —PSALM 24:3–4

> *Blessed are the pure in heart, for they will see God.*
>
> —MATTHEW 5:8

> *Let us draw near to God with a sincere heart and with the full assurance that faith brings, having our hearts sprinkled to cleanse us from a guilty conscience and having our bodies washed with pure water.*
>
> —HEBREWS 10:22

A clean heart, or a pure, unadulterated heart, is a requirement for living synced. Jesus kept His heart pure—unmixed, focused. One whose heart is not clean can't enter into the intimate fellowship with the Father that the Father so desires. A heart with divided affections is a barrier between you and God. He is not satisfied with a half-hearted love. "Do not worship any other god, for the LORD, whose name is Jealous, is a jealous God" (Exodus 34:14). When Jesus enters your life in His fullness, His presence sweeps clean every crack and crevice of your being.

IT'S ALL ABOUT THE HEART

God invites you to draw near with a sincere heart. What is a sincere heart and how do you get one? The word *heart* is popularly used to indicate a mushy emotionalism: softhearted, brokenhearted, big-hearted, and so forth. However, when God refers to the heart, He is referring to the whole inner person. In its scriptural context, the heart is the seat of the intellect, the will, the personality, and the emotions. It would make sense to translate it as *mind*. Scripture says, "Draw near to God with a sincere heart" (Hebrews 10:22). A sincere, true, authentic, genuine heart is a heart that is what it purports to be. It is a heart that is unmixed, like pure gold or pure silver, unalloyed with other elements. Sören Kierkegaard has expressed it best: "Purity of heart is to will one thing." It is not the mighty in intellect who will see God but the pure in heart.

You cannot purify your own heart. You do not have the ability to give God a sincere heart. Your heart is wicked and deceitful, and you cannot fully understand it. We are experts at deceiving ourselves with rationalizations and denials. Our hearts have an elaborate set of defense mechanisms that operate automatically to disguise and hide our true selves. "The heart is deceitful above all things and beyond cure. Who can understand it?" (Jeremiah 17:9). Truth, or authenticity, is buried under layers and layers of pretense. We do not know the truth about ourselves. This is the human condition. We are helpless to even diagnose, let alone treat, our own desperate condition.

If God demands a pure heart, and you cannot achieve a pure heart, how will this dilemma be resolved? There is only one way to a pure heart—invite the Refiner's Fire into your life.

> *But who can endure the day of his coming? Who can stand when he appears? For he will be like a refiner's fire or a launderer's soap. He will sit as a refiner and purifier of silver; he will purify the Levites and refine them like gold and silver.*
>
> —MALACHI 3:2–3

Silver is usually found in an ore alloyed with other less valuable elements. The silver must be extracted and refined from all impurities to be considered pure silver. Impurities in a metal diminish its strength and dilute its value. By use of heat or chemicals, a refiner removes impurities and alloys so that pure silver is all that remains. The Refiner's Fire—Jesus—enters your life as a heart-purifier. He refines you like silver. He isolates and then eliminates impurities. He washes you with launderer's soap. In biblical times, launderer's soap was used to clean clothing. Garments were soaked in launderer's soap to loosen the dirt and then stomped on to release the loosened grime. Sometimes God uses adverse circumstances as a purifying agent. He may use the fiery heat of His holiness to convict you of sin and draw you toward righteousness. Every person and every circumstance He allows into your life can be used to purify you. Nothing is wasted, nothing is an accident. The purifying process, if momentarily painful or uncomfortable, is producing something eternal that far outweighs the temporary discomfort.

For our light and momentary troubles are achieving for us an eternal glory that far outweighs them all. So we fix our eyes not on what is seen, but on what is unseen, since what is seen is temporary, but what is unseen is eternal.

—2 CORINTHIANS 4:17–18

LIVING SYNCED: SOMETIMES NOT ENOUGH IS MORE THAN ENOUGH

Let me illustrate from my own life. I had been financially comfortable all my life. There were very few things I wanted that I could not afford. I thought I did not love material things. I thought I could be perfectly happy with or without them, that they did not add to my feeling of value. The truth was hidden and disguised by my deceitful heart. However, in the process of purifying me, God needed to expose the lurking, ugly reality. My husband went through a long period of unemployment. Material things were unavailable to me. I found that I loved them very much. I found that my self-esteem was built on very shaky ground.

Not only does God want to expose impurities, but He also wants to remove them. As He brought my problem to the surface in the crucible of my circumstances, He also began to clean it away. He cleansed me by allowing me to experience His love and care with such clarity that I saw everything else in a new light. For two years, nothing changed in my circumstances, but everything changed in my perception. He thrust a circumstance on me so that He could build a sincere heart within me.

This is only one example. God has used people and circumstances to cause me to come face-to-face with the truth. He builds authenticity into my life. Although it is a difficult transition, He causes me to love the truth more than the lie. My first reaction is to hide from the truth and cling to the lie. The lie always makes me look better to myself. At first, I always love the darkness more than the light. I feel exposed in the light. Then He reminds me that He is the Light and the Truth, and that He has come to set me free. It is His great mercy and love for me that brings Him into my life as the Refiner's Fire.

I am learning to welcome tribulation and to treat it as a friend. Trials are God's detergents. He works in me to create the desire for Him, whatever the cost. "Not only so, but we also glory in our sufferings, because we know that suffering produces perseverance; perseverance, character; and character, hope. And hope does not put us to shame" (Romans 5:3–5). It is His mighty power in my inner person that is burning away everything that is not Him and every rival for my affections, causing me to will one thing. This refining and purifying has one goal: to free me to be what I am called to be. "Not that I have already obtained all this, or have already arrived at my goal, but I press on to take hold of that for which Christ Jesus took hold of me" (Philippians 3:12). And for what purpose did Christ take hold of me? To establish the kingdom of God on earth through prayer. To live synced to His heart so that His heart is reproduced in me and flows through me.

A SPRINKLE IS A DELUGE

"Draw near with a heart sprinkled clean." God wants us to draw near with a heart sprinkled clean from an evil conscience (Hebrews

10:22). The phrase "sprinkled clean" refers to the Old Covenant requirements of being cleansed by blood. The sprinkling of blood inaugurated the Old Covenant (9:18–22) and was used consistently throughout the Old Testament to signify cleansing.

Drawing on modern understanding of human physiology, we know that blood does not cleanse from the outside but from the inside. Blood is the essence of life. It is because the blood represents the vitality, the life and being, that it makes atonement. "For the life of a creature is in the blood, and I have given it to you to make atonement for yourselves on the altar; it is the blood that makes atonement for one's life" (Leviticus 17:11). His blood—His material, physical blood that flowed in His body and was shed at the Cross— was a picture of His life force, His Holy Spirit, which flows through our spirits, cleansing us. "And the blood of Jesus, his Son, purifies us from all sin" (1 John 1:7). You are continuously being cleansed of all unrighteousness because He lives His life through you. His life is always flowing through you, flushing away impurities. As our blood flows through our physical bodies, it carries away toxins.

When God instituted the New Covenant, He changed His whole theater of operation from outside man to inside man. His law is not written on stone tablets but on the tablets of the heart. The blood that sealed the first covenant was the blood of animals. It could not really cleanse but could only symbolize cleansing. The only way for that blood to be applied was by sprinkling it externally. The blood of the eternal covenant is the blood of Christ. His blood—His life, in Spirit form, is not sprinkled on but flowing through. The cleansing life flow has been transfused into us. The life Christ lives through you is not the life He once lived in the flesh, encapsulated in time. He lives His resurrected life in you; His present-tense life, His glorified life. He does not diminish Himself to fit your limitations, but He expands you to accommodate His unlimited capacities.

In letting go of the old life to embrace the Christ-life, you learn that you can do all things through Christ who strengthens you (Philippians 4:13). I don't mean that you are all-powerful and can do anything you set out to do. I mean you are empowered to do anything God appoints you to do. He will call on you to do far more than you could ever do in your own power. The uninterrupted flow of Christ's life through you keeps you in unbroken fellowship with Him as He is in unbroken fellowship with the Father: "I in them and you in me" (John 17:23). His cleansing is always active within you. He is always working in you to create a clean heart.

A CLEAN HEART

To experience a clean heart, a sincere heart, you must willingly submit yourself to God for the purpose of having sin exposed and expunged. You must come to the conclusion that you cannot purify your own heart and that you are helpless in this matter. This is an important part of the faith journey. God gave the law for just this purpose.

The law is to have two functions in the life of the believer. First, the law shows you your sin by clarifying the standard of righteousness. "I would not have known what sin was had it not been for the law. For I would not have known what coveting really was if the law had not said, 'You shall not covet'" (Romans 7:7). Second, the law exposes your powerlessness over sin. In seeking to keep the law, you will fail time and again. You will be unable to live up to God's standard. "For I know that good itself does not dwell in me, that is, in my sinful nature. For I have the desire to do what is good, but I cannot carry it out" (v. 18).

Have you reached this conclusion? Do you know for certain that, no matter how firm your purpose or how good your intentions, you cannot fulfill the standard of righteousness? Have you given up? Giving up is hard. It's hard to admit that you're powerless. It's even harder to relinquish your whole self, which is required for a pure heart.

Let me explain what I mean. I want to be cleansed of my sins. My sins are inconvenient to me. They show me for what I am. They diminish my life. I want God to come into my life and patch up the holes and put on a new coat of paint. I want my life to look bright and shiny and to feel good. But that's not His way. Do I want Him to tear down the old and build something new? Do I want to die to myself and live to Him? Do I want Him to deal with the very root of my sins, my self-rule?

He wants to take out my old heart and put in a new heart. My old heart is set on my gain. At its very best, no matter how good my actions, how righteous my thoughts, my heart is set on my gain. I come to God for His favors, for His blessings, for His forgiveness, for my own sake. No matter how much I want to change, I can't. I can't change my heart.

I will give you a new heart and put a new spirit in you;
I will remove from you your heart of stone and give you a

heart of flesh. And I will put my Spirit in you and move
you to follow my decrees and be careful to keep my laws.

—EZEKIEL 36:26–27

A heart transplant. A blood transfusion. A completely new creation.
This is the radical work of Christ in me. This is the New Covenant
way. Free from the external law, bound to the "living law." The law
once engraved on stone, now engraved in my inner person. Now
everything is changed. The law is not a document but a person. Jesus
is the embodiment of the law. His life is flowing through you. The law
is not a burden to which you are bound or by which you are inhibited.
Rather He is the freedom you are seeking. He is the escape from the
sin that had bound you. As you live your daily life, the Living Law
Himself guides you from within. It is the Holy Spirit who makes the
law real in your experience.

To live synced, you must be always yielded and receptive. You
must accept your own helplessness and inability to change. Once
you've learned the ways of the kingdom, you can, like Paul, boast
about your weaknesses, that the power of Christ may dwell in you.
Be well content with your weaknesses, for when you are weak, then
you are strong.

Living synced to Jesus allows Him the access He wants to create an incorruptible heart in you. He wants a heart that is not conformed to the world but transformed by the Spirit (Romans 12:2).
Draw near to God with a genuine heart, in the full assurance of faith,
and with a heart cleansed by the blood of Christ (James 4:8). A pure
heart. A synced life.

PASS IT ON

The second part of the petition is "as we also have forgiven our debtors." When we experience forgiveness, then we are more disposed to forgive. Receiving forgiveness is the benefit we gain from His death on the Cross. We are forgiven freely and joyfully for every sin of every kind. In response, we are to forgive everybody for everything.

Every act of obedience is a step toward greater freedom. Jesus said, "When you stand praying, if you hold anything against anyone, forgive them" (Mark 11:25). This is a difficult thing to obey because our sinful nature—our spiritual genetics—predisposes us to hold a grudge or exact revenge. The command to forgive *everyone* for *everything* opposes our human nature. This command to forgive seems like a heavy burden to bear. It seems too much to ask.

Having heard the command of Christ, you are now faced with a choice. Will you be a slave to anger and bitterness, which will lead to your own destruction? Or will you forgive and be freed from the too heavy, emotionally crippling burden of anger? Will you draw on the resources of your human nature or will you draw on the resources of the kingdom of God? You choose.

There are many levels of offense, all of which must be forgiven for your own good. However, I know that some of you reading this book have been betrayed or abused and are suffering great inner pain. That pain may be intensified by feelings of guilt brought on by knowing you should be able to forgive. Remember several things. Forgiveness is a process. It is not accomplished by saying a few magic words. It is a process initiated and completed by Christ in you. You do not have a deadline to meet. Your process may be different from anyone else's. You may be encouraged or guided by the similar experiences of others, but don't be dictated by them. Be patient with yourself. Remember that God has undertaken the work within you and the responsibility is His. Once you have entered the process by yielding yourself to His working, you have fulfilled His commandment.

You can't begin the process until you can face your anger and hurt honestly. Don't be afraid to take your pain and anger to God. He won't reject you. He is not fragile. You can ask Him your hardest questions. You can lay your blackest anger out before Him, even when some of that anger is directed at Him. He will take you by the hand and walk you step-by-step through the process of forgiveness and inner healing. He will put all the pieces back together again. As He does, He will show you Himself in new and wonderful ways. He will use even the most awful events for your good. Your pain and the subsequent healing and transformation will teach you how to live synced, walking and living in the flow of His provision.

When God leads you through fire, it is not a destroying fire but a cleansing fire. It will not consume you. It will refine you. He is shaping you, like an artist shapes a sculpture. The fire will set the work He has done so the shape will be stable. Never be afraid of the fire.

IT'S THE LITTLE THINGS

The truth is that many—maybe most—of the offenses for which we hold a grudge are small infractions, slights, and perceived insults. Most of the time, the offense was a blow to our pride in some way. Someone didn't treat us as we thought we deserved, failed to acknowledge something, or said something that we considered demeaning.

No real harm done, other than to our own pride. We often assume they intended offense, when in reality they may not even know we were offended. If the offender is in our lives, then we probably store up a collection of insults and take them out and inventory them from time to time. Each new offense has grown in its impact because it is added to an already smoldering stack of similar events.

This is the way most of us are nurturing bitterness in our lives, and it is harmful to us. It is toxic. We have to let these things go before they eat away at our hearts and harden our hearts toward the Holy Spirit's influence. Holding on to bitterness is sin. We are warned away from it.

I wrote about this in *Live a Praying Life*® as follows:

> He will not settle for leaving "just a little bit" of sin to diminish your life. He is always rooting it out, exposing it, bringing it into the light. He wants you to forgive *everyone* for *everything* because He loves you obsessively and wants to see you reach your potential.
>
> God, expressing Himself through Christ, is the model for how we are to forgive. *"Be kind and compassionate to one another, forgiving each other, just as in Christ God forgave you"* (Ephesians 4:32). How does God forgive?
>
> 1. He forgives completely. *"For I will forgive their wickedness and will remember their sins no more"* (Hebrews 8:12). *"And where these have been forgiven, sacrifice for sin is no longer necessary"* (10:18).
>
> 2. He forgives us when we didn't deserve it and didn't even desire it. *"But God demonstrates his own love for us*

in this: While we were still sinners, Christ died for us" (Romans 5:8).

3. He began the forgiving process even while the offense was in progress. *"When they came to the place called the Skull, they crucified him there, along with the criminals—one on his right, the other on his left. Jesus said, 'Father, forgive them, for they do not know what they are doing.' And they divided up his clothes by casting lots"* (Luke 23:33–34).

I have found Jesus' words, "they do not know what they are doing," to be extremely important in learning to forgive. I believe this is nearly always true. The one who offended you does not really know what he or she is doing. A large percentage of the offenses against us are entirely unintentional. Most of the time, your offender has no idea how you have perceived his actions or words. You, in fact, have hurt or offended others unintentionally. How many of the hurts that you are struggling with are really your perceptions of a situation or a comment? How much of the anger you have against others is really the result of feelings, attitudes, or intentions that you are projecting on other people? Forgive them. They do not know what they are doing.

Even when a person's words or actions are deliberately unkind or harsh, as were the soldiers' who were crucifying Jesus, the person does not fully understand the ramifications. Strange as it seems, even a person who appears to be intentionally harming you has been blinded by the enemy to the whole picture. Your enemy is not flesh and blood. The human heart is deceitful—able to fool itself. Forgive him. Forgive her. Let it go. They do not know what they are doing.

LIVING SYNCED: MISSION IMPOSSIBLE

Author Carol Kent has let her experience transform her and, through her, the lives of many as she tells her heartbreaking story of her only child, her son Jason. Jason, in an act that is a complete aberration of his whole life and character, committed a murder, believing himself to be protecting his stepdaughters, and received a life sentence without possibility of parole. Carol tells the story in her book *A New Kind of Normal*. The following story proceeds from that. Carol tells this story of synced living that leads to forgiveness in *Between a Rock and a Grace Place*.

After an event where Carol had told her story, a woman named Tammy Wilson emailed her. Tammy's mother had been murdered in the course of a robbery at her workplace by a young man named Matt Rodriguez. Matt was convicted and given a life sentence for his crime. As she healed from her loss, Tammy began to pray for Matt, not knowing anything about him personally. She allowed the living, present Jesus to forgive him through her. She contacted Carol because she had looked up Jason and found that he was incarcerated at Hardee Correctional Institution in Bowling Green, Florida, which was where her mother's murderer was also incarcerated. Tammy had written to Matt over the years, but had never sent the letters. She wondered if Carol would have any way to get her letters to Matt.

Matt, it happens, is one of Jason's best friends. He has turned his life around and is a committed follower of Jesus and an influential encourager among the inmates. To encapsulate a story that has many God details in it, Tammy and Matt have connected, and grace flows in abundance as their story continues.

Who could have woven all those elements together to create such a story? I mentioned earlier, when you are living synced, many of your stories have "it just happened" in them.

Carol summarizes this event with the following thoughts:

> While being forgiven and granted the grace to let go of personal guilt is a freeing experience, the act of forgiving and letting go of resentment is every bit as profound in its power to transform the person who has been harmed. The story of a person who forgives from the heart contains a significant element of surprise in itself, simply because human beings, by nature, are not very forgiving. When we are deeply wounded, our natural and understandable reaction is to lash out at the person or situation that has harmed us—or to retreat, protect ourselves, and silently punish the offender by withholding grace. What we sometimes don't realize, however, is that by keeping the fire burning under our resentment and holding on to our hurt and anger, we actually increase our suffering and trap ourselves in a cycle of blame and sorrow that can make our lives a living hell.

To sync your heart with Jesus' heart, receive His forgiveness and then pass it on. Do not refuse to acknowledge sin or forsake sin that the Holy Spirit has identified in you. Refusing to accept and receive the forgiveness He paid so high a price for you to have will keep you from the full force of His life and the total experience of His love for you. It won't lessen His love for you, but it will rob you of fully knowing it in your experience. On the other hand, to hang onto bitterness and anger toward someone who has hurt or offended you will keep you arm's length from His heart—not because He has removed Himself from you, but rather because you have chosen to erect and protect a barrier around your own heart. His command for you to forgive is an invitation to live with your heart synced to His love.

PROVEN

Jesus taught His disciples to pray as He prayed, "Lead us not into temptation, but deliver us from the evil one" (Matthew 6:13). This begs the question, does God lead us into temptation?

The word translated "temptation" also means "testing." God does not tempt us (entice us to sin) according to James 1:13, but He does allow testing in our lives. Let's think about His testing for a minute.

James 1:2–4 (author's words added) says:

> *Consider it pure joy, my brothers and sisters, whenever you face trials [testing] of many kinds, because you know that the testing of your faith produces perseverance. Let perseverance finish its work so that you may be mature and complete, not lacking anything.*

Why does God need to test our faith? Is He not sure how much faith we have until He has devised a test to evaluate us? And, why would He need to test Jesus' faith?

It means to put it to the test to prove it is strong and true. Untried faith is unproven faith. The trying of faith is necessary to validate its authenticity and to demonstrate its power. Jesus experienced intense times of testing. Not to see if He was genuine but to prove that He was genuine. I've described it like this in my book *Live a Praying Life*®:

> When God brings waiting periods into your life it is for only one reason: so that you can test-drive your faith. If I were planning to buy a car, I could research my purchase and decide what car I wanted—what make and model, what color, what add-on features. I could know everything about the car I want except how it handles in my hands. Not until I get behind the wheel and drive it for myself will I know the feel of the car. I have to drive it myself before I can know exactly how to adjust the seat and the mirrors, or how much pressure I have to put on the brake pedal to bring it to smooth stop, or exactly how I have to turn the steering wheel to get exactly the right angle when I turn. I won't make my final purchase until I've handled the car myself—until I've test-driven it. It's the same way with your faith. You can study faith. You can memorize verses about faith. You can learn slick, pithy definitions about faith. But until you have the opportunity to test-drive your own faith, you will never know how it handles in your hands. James says that God "tests" our faith. Does that mean He puts it to the test so that He can see how much faith you have? Or does He put it to the test so that you can see how faith operates? The word "test" really

means "to prove." God knows everything about you and everything that's in your heart. In fact, He knows it better than you do. He doesn't have to devise a test that will tell Him about your faith. He is proving your faith to you! Peter says the same thing: "These [i.e., trials] have come so that your faith—of greater worth than gold, which perishes even though refined by fire—may be proved genuine and may result in praise, glory and honor when Jesus Christ is revealed" (1 Peter 1:7, author's words added).

When God allows you to test-drive your faith over and over again, you learn how to operate in faith with confidence. You become a mature and seasoned faith-walker. Mature faith has deep roots. It is not easily shaken. The person with mature faith is steady and tenacious. He has what James calls "perseverance," the ability to go the distance.

He tests to prove. Every time Jesus was put to the test, He proved Himself genuine. When God allows you to be tested by circumstances, it is not so that He can give you a grade but so that He can prove to you that He is faithful and that He has provided you all the resources of heaven for your situation. He proves that you can live synced to the heart of Jesus, and through Him, you have everything you need when you need it.

This petition, however, is not a request to be spared from the testing that is necessary to produce the ultimate outcome of living synced; rather, it is a request to be protected from any challenge that does not have a productive purpose. This is a prayer for protection from situations that will lead to failure instead of strength and refinement. Jesus prayed, "My prayer is not that you take them out of the world but that you protect them from the evil one" (John 17:15).

This petition, taught by Jesus Himself, assures us that any challenging situations that God allows in our lives will have a good outcome, and any situation that would be destructive will be filtered out. When Jesus prayed in the Garden of Gethsemane, "Father, if you are willing, take this cup from me; yet not my will, but yours be done" (Luke 22:42), He was saying, "If this is necessary for You to accomplish Your will, then I yield." When you have asked to not be led into unnecessary testing, then you know that every situation has filtered out any testing that has no eternal purpose—any testing that is not outweighed by the outcome it produces. "And we know that in all things God works for the good of those who love him, who have been called according to his purpose" (Romans 8:28).

"'Why are you sleeping?' [Jesus] asked them. 'Get up and pray so that you will not fall into temptation'" (Luke 22:46, author's words added). During those emotionally charged hours before His arrest, Jesus urgently reminded His disciples to strengthen themselves through prayer against the onslaught of testing headed their way. That openness to the flow of God's power and provision—syncing your heart with His—would provide the victory in the moment of testing. When the moment came for proving what was on the inside, the battle the disciples faced could have been won in the prayer that preceded it. At least twice during His prayer vigil, Jesus admonished His disciples with those words. Don't you think that this gives us some insight into the spiritual battle in which Jesus was engaged during His Gethsemane hours? The moment was approaching for which His whole purpose in coming to earth would be put to the test. His mission would be tested and proven. Jesus, during His period of agonized praying, received from the Father the strength, assurance, endurance, courage, and confidence to face the temptation—more accurately, the trial—and not fall. His mental, emotional, and spiritual serenity throughout His crucifixion experience was birthed in the hours of prayer and the life of prayer that preceded it. "The Lord knows how to rescue the godly from trials" (2 Peter 2:9).

"Lead us not into temptation, but deliver us from the evil one" (Matthew 6:13). Never will Satan's plans accomplish Satan's goals. His goal is to kill, steal, and destroy, but His actions will never produce his desired result. God will use the best schemes of the evil one to accomplish His eternal plan.

Have you ever thought about how detailed and exactly timed the arrest, trial, crucifixion, burial, and Resurrection of Jesus was? The exact timing had been established before the world began. God gave an elaborate and explicit picture of the timing when He established the feasts in the Old Covenant, generations before the event occurred in history. Every detail of His ordeal was laid out in the beginning. Jesus had to be on the Cross and dead by sundown on Passover because He is the Paschal Lamb. The exact incident had to occur by twilight on the fourteenth day of the first month, the month of Nisan. He had to be in the ground before 6:00 p.m. because He is the whole burnt offering sacrifice for the nation. He had to be resurrected on the third day, the day following the Sabbath, the Feast of Firstfruits, because He is the Firstfruits of the Spirit. He had to be resurrected after sunset and before sunrise for His Resurrection to fall within the prescribed day . . . God's timetable was exact. He did not deviate from it at all. However, look at the events that put everything on this timetable.

> *Now the Feast of Unleavened Bread, called the Passover,*
> *was approaching, and the chief priests and the teachers of*
> *the law were looking for some way to get rid of Jesus, for*
> *they were afraid of the people.*
>
> —LUKE 22:1–2

At exactly the right moment, Jesus' enemies began to act on their festering hatred and fear of Him.

Until that moment, Jesus had always said, "My time is not yet here" (John 7:6). Until that time, His enemies' schemes could not succeed. Because of their impatience to finish the deed before the Sabbath, Jesus' enemies called an unusual meeting of the Sanhedrin, then they woke Pilate, then Herod (who just happened to be in Jerusalem at that time), and finally Pilate again. What should have taken several days—at least—was railroaded through by enemies of God. Because of their manipulation of events, every event occurred exactly on God's predetermined timetable, the timetable He had planned from the beginning of time and announced early in Israel's history. "The LORD works out everything to its proper end—even the wicked for a day of disaster" (Proverbs 16:4).

Even Satan is nothing more than a pawn in God's hands. Observe Satan's part in God's plan: between the temptation of Jesus and His crucifixion, Satan was watching for a perfect time to carry out his own agenda. "When the devil had finished all this tempting, he left him until an opportune time" (Luke 4:13). Now—at this exact moment—Satan sees his opportune time. "Then Satan entered Judas . . . And Judas went to the chief priests and the officers of the temple guard and discussed with them how he might betray Jesus. . . . He . . . watched for an opportunity to hand Jesus over to them when no crowd was present" (22:3–6). Satan had found the opportune time for which he had been watching. The irony is that it was God's opportune time, not Satan's.

Jesus, living synced to the Father's heart, could trust that nothing in His horrendous, unspeakable ordeal was other than what was essential to accomplish God's purpose. He knew that His anguish and torment would yield our salvation. The darkness He would walk through would give way to light; and the mourning would turn to dancing.

LIVING SYNCED: PROVEN TRUE

Karla Faye Tucker, the first woman executed in Texas in more than 100 years, became an evangelist for Christ during her 14-year imprisonment on death row. In her book *Karla Faye Tucker Set Free*, author Linda Strom tells Karla's story. I'm going to summarize a small portion of that story to illustrate synced living that emerged out of great evil. The enemy's plans were thwarted and God's plans were fulfilled when Karla synced her life to His.

The story of Karla's life before prison and her vicious, brutal crime starts out as the story of a person hopelessly imprisoned in a life defined by bad choices and one central unthinkable act of violence. Karla, in a drugged tirade with her boyfriend, murdered Jerry

Lynn Dean and Debora Thorton with a pickax in a robbery attempt gone horribly wrong.

Jerry had a sister named Peggy. Let's start Karla's story with her. Peggy and her husband, Fred, were unsaved and uninterested in anything about God. Fred was vice president of a national company that had a warehouse full of goods that he needed to dispose of. He arranged to donate them to a church and talked Peggy into going with him on a Sunday so the church could thank them. That day changed everything in their lives and they came to the Lord and began to grow in Him. When Peggy's youngest brother was murdered, God had laid the groundwork. The murder was front-page news day and night and the murderers had not yet been apprehended. Peggy was dealing with the grief and the horror of her situation and struggling through it. Her pastor and church prayed with her, and she committed herself to forgiving these assailants and began to pray for their salvation, not knowing who they were or anything about them.

In *Karla Faye Tucker Set Free,* Peggy says:

> There is power in a praying church. Karla and Danny were apprehended that night, thirty-five days after Jerry's murder. The next morning I discovered they were arrested. But I had no sooner given it up to the Lord, and my anger started all over again. Now there were faces. Finally I had someone to put my hatred on. I had from Thursday to Sunday to hate. Then I said, "No, I am not going to do this. God has set me free and what God has freed is free indeed." I'm still free.

Now let's jump to Karla. Hardened, remorseless, angry. She was being held in Harris County Jail in Houston awaiting trial where it was fairly certain that she would receive the death penalty. Here is Karla's story in her own words from *Karla Faye Tucker Set Free*:

> I was awaiting my trial when a prison ministry group visited the jail. I just went to see what it was like. They were putting on a puppet show. When I walked through the door, my mouth kind of dropped. I felt something that I had never felt before. I know now that it was the presence of God. I remember looking at the ministry team and I don't know how I knew they had been where I was at, but inside I knew they had been in jails and prisons, been into prostitution, violence, and drugs. I remember thinking, *I want to feel what they're feeling*. They had a peace and a joy—something that was real. I had never seen that in anybody.
>
> That night when the service was over I snuck a Bible. I wasn't aware that they gave Bibles out freely to help people in jail, so I thought I was stealing it. I took it with me to my cell and hid back in the corner.
>
> I opened the Bible and started reading. I don't know how long it took, but I remember that I was kneeling on the floor, crying, asking God to come into my heart and forgive me for what I had done.
>
> I don't know that I felt forgiven at that point, but I do know I felt love. I knew that no matter what I had done I was loved, just like that, just like I was. That's

when the whole weight of what I did fell on me. I realized for the first time that I had brutally murdered two people and there were people out there hurting because of me. Yet God was saying, "I love you." It was supernatural. I don't really know how to explain it. At that moment, He reached down inside of me and ripped out that violence at the very roots and poured Himself in.

I knew then that I had to tell the truth about everything. Before I knew the Lord, I didn't care what anybody else felt or thought. I didn't want to tell what had happened for fear of what the consequences would be. When the Lord came into my life and changed me, I realized I couldn't count the cost of my own life. I had to tell the truth about everything. I was not fearful of what man could do to me.

Karla spent 14 years on death row and was executed. By all accounts she went to her death humming hymns, expressing love and concern for others, and at peace. During those 14 years, she influenced many. She led many to the Lord and encouraged other women on death row. Author Linda Strom developed and grew an amazing ministry reaching out to prisoners called Discipleship Unlimited. I have had many opportunities to minister in the prisons with Linda, and it is one of the most meaningful and moving experiences in ministry I have ever had. All this traces back to a moment when a woman whom we would have categorized as one of society's losers was won by Jesus.

When we are living synced, Jesus is orchestrating the most impossible situations, merging seemingly random events, converging lives that would never connect any other way. All of it seems to be random; it just flows.

And Jesus is winning the day. When He prayed, "Lead us not into temptation, but deliver us from the evil one," He saw it in His own life. He knew by experience that it worked. That is why He taught His disciples to pray just exactly that.

CONCLUSION

Jesus showed us how we could live synced to His heart the same way He lived synced to the Father's heart. No more struggling and agonizing over trying to find His will. Living synced, His will finds you. No more wondering and second guessing about decisions because the right choice presents itself. Living at rest, in a soul Sabbath, in the flow of His provision—living synced.

The key to keeping your heart connected to His is keeping your eyes fixed on Jesus (Hebrews 12:2) like synchronized swimmers who train by keeping their eyes glued to each other until their synchronization flows naturally.

> *My eyes are ever on the LORD, for only he will release my feet from the snare.*
>
> —PSALM 25:15

In His Model Prayer, Jesus showed us the way He prayed during His days on earth that kept His heart synced. He gave us the secret for how powerful living and powerful praying are two parts of one whole. Now, as you reach the end of this book, my prayer is that you are chomping at the bit to let Jesus show you more every day about how to live synced.

Live A Praying Life® Series

Whether for your own individual study, or small group/church Bible study, the *Live a Praying Life*® series is timeless. National best-selling author Jennifer Kennedy Dean takes you back to the biblical basics of prayer, cleaning out myths about prayer to rev up a powerful, ongoing connection to God that can invigorate every aspect of a Christian's life.

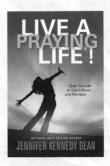

Live a Praying Life®!
JENNIFER KENNEDY DEAN

ISBN 13: 978-1-59669-436-1

$14.99

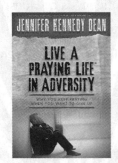

Live a Praying Life® in Adversity
JENNIFER KENNEDY DEAN

ISBN 13: 978-1-59669-410-1

$11.99

Live a Praying Life® Journal
JENNIFER KENNEDY DEAN

ISBN 13: 978-1-59669-289-3

$14.99

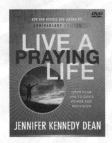

Live a Praying Life® DVD Leader's Kit (Anniversary Edition)
JENNIFER KENNEDY DEAN

ISBN 13: 978-1-59669-290-9

$99.99

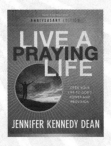

Live a Praying Life® Workbook (Anniversary Edition)
JENNIFER KENNEDY DEAN

ISBN 13: 978-1-59669-291-6

$14.99

For information about our books and authors, visit NewHopePublishers.com. Experience sample chapters, author videos, interviews, and more!

Remedy your prayer life!

Nationally recognized prayer leader Jennifer Kennedy Dean helps you discover that "prayer fatigue" is a widespread spiritual condition. *Prayer Fatigue* takes a look at each of the ten symptoms of this spiritual disease and offers practical and scriptural remedies to revitalize your prayer life.

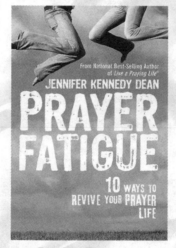

Prayer Fatigue

JENNIFER KENNEDY DEAN

ISBN 13: 978-1-59669-426-2

$15.99

For information about our books and authors, visit
NewHopePublishers.com. Experience sample chapters,
author videos, interviews, and more!

365 Days with the God Who Gives Us His Attention...

Provoking us to intimate, fulfilling conversation, *Conversations with the Most High* will help prepare the Christian believer's heart to enter the throne room of God. A blessed resource each day, 365 devotions steeped in Scripture engage our focus and prompt us in communication with the God who loves us.

Peppered with quotes from notable, historical experts on prayer, the short and timely narratives make for excellent discussion starters and listening gauges for conversation with God.

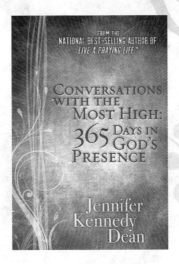

Conversations with the Most High

JENNIFER KENNEDY DEAN

ISBN 13: 978-1-59669-393-7

$16.99

For information about our books and authors, visit
NewHopePublishers.com. Experience sample chapters,
author videos, interviews, and more!

Experience freedom, power, and peace.

Clothed with Power helps you explore how the Holy Spirit is at work in every area of your life. Designed as a six-week interactive study, national best-selling author and prayer expert Jennifer Kennedy Dean uses the symbolism of the Old Testament priests' garments to show you anew how your salvation has always been a part of God's redemptive plan. And, how it is through that salvation that the Holy Spirit is the living Jesus in you now—making you fit for heaven's work here on earth.

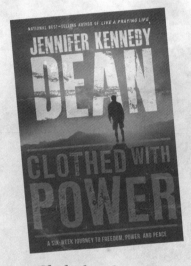

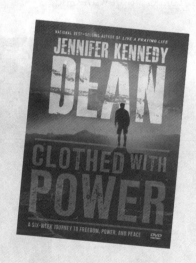

Clothed with Power
JENNIFER KENNEDY DEAN
ISBN 13: 978-1-59669-373-9
$14.99

*An accompanying DVD to this study is also available.
ISBN 13: 978-1-59669-381-4
$29.99

For information about our books and authors, visit NewHopePublishers.com. Experience sample chapters, author videos, interviews, and more!